Toddler Bites Publishing

A to Z Toddler & Preschool Curriculum

Please email info@toddlerbitesonline.com for more information.
The author is available to speak and conduct workshops.

Please visit the Toddler Bites blog for ideas added almost daily:
www.toddlerbitesblog.wordpress.com

Copyright © 2011 Kathy Hutto

A
Color: Red
Number: 1
Shape: Circle
Scripture: Children, obey your parents in the Lord: for this is right. Ephesians 6:1

Theme: **Apples**

Bible: Adam & Eve
- Scripture: Children, obey your parents in the Lord: for this is right. Ephesians 6:1
- Tell story of Adam and Eve. Keep it simple: God made Adam. God made Eve. God Made Me. God said don't eat fruit from one tree. Adam and Eve did not obey. Bible Concept: We must obey.
- As you cover the theme apples, remind toddler of the Bible concept this week: We must obey.
- Play in the sandbox or make a homemade sandbox for this week if you don't have one. Home stores sell bags of play sand for only $4. Fill a large rubber maid "under the bed storage box" with the sand.   Use this sand play to teach that God formed Adam out of dirt.

Theme Learning:
> Talk about how apples grow. Apple trees grow from seeds and apples grow on apple trees. Discuss the different colors apples can be: red, yellow, or green. Ask, "Which color do you like the best?" Guess how many seeds are in the apple. Cut open an apple and show some seeds from the inside. Discuss what they look like, what color they are, what shape they are in (teardrop). Plant an apple seed in a paper cup or small pot and discuss what the seed needs in order to to grow: soil, water, sun.

Letter Skills:
- Say It: A says "a" like "achoo"
- Play a Game: Give your toddler a Kleenex and have him practice saying "a..a..a..choo!" Glue Kleenex to hand (page included at back)
- Decorate blank A with fingerprint ants using black washable paint or black stamp pad. Just draw on legs and antennae to their fingerprints using black marker.
- Letter "A" Box: In advance fill an empty wet wipes container or shoe box with items found around the house that begin with the letter a; have child add to the box through the week as they find things that start with the /a/ sound (Ex. animal cracker, apple, alligator toy, etc.) Enrichment: look for things with "a" in middle

Math:
- String Apple Jacks cereal onto yarn (to avoid frustration, be sure to use extra wide tape on the end of the yarn so it doesn't fray and so that it is easier for your toddler to manipulate)
- Guess how many seeds in a apple; cut open and count out loud to your toddler

- Glue black seeds (from above activity or cut out from black construction paper) to a red construction paper apple; give the seeds to your toddler one at a time and make him say one…one…one

Shape Practice:
- Have toddler put red circular price stickers found in Office Supply store on Handprint Apple Trees (see Art section below)
- Shape Hunt: Look around the house for circles. Examples: oatmeal container lid, clock on wall, favorite DVD, etc.
- Teach child to draw circles. Guide his/her hand around and around while holding crayon making circles on paper. Trace around a coffee can lid (or other lid)

Color:
- Sort red, green, and yellow construction paper apples cutouts
- Play with red play dough and apple shaped cookie cutter
- Sort red, green, and yellow apples: put red, green, and yellow construction paper sheets in front of child. Let him sort apples onto correct paper.

Art:

- Apple Stamping: Use apple you cut in half during Math; put red paint on paper plate, dip apple halves cut side down into paint and let child stamp apple prints on white paper. *Enrichment: stamp apple prints on canvas apron bought in craft section of large stores; give the apron as a gift to a deserving widow, elderly neighbor, hard working church kitchen staff member, or save as special surprise for Grandmother on Grandparent's Day (first Sunday of September)
- Stained Glass Apples: cut apple shape from clear contact paper; peel to reveal sticky side; have child place red, green, yellow tissue paper squares onto the sticky contact paper; cover with another contact paper apple cutout to seal; punch hole and tie yard for hanging on window in kitchen

- Apple Tree Handprint Tree: paint child's hand and part of arm using washable brown paint and large paintbrush; have him press hand/arm onto white construction paper; when dry, add red circular stickers for apples (see Shape Practice section above)

Story Time:
- <u>How Do Apples Grow</u> by Betsy Maestro
- <u>The Apple Pie Tree</u> by Zoe Hall
- <u>The Giving Tree</u> by Shel Silverstein
- <u>Ten Apples Up on Top</u> by Dr. Seuss

Music:
- Use construction paper apple cutouts from Color section above. Sing the song below and at the end, throw the apples into the air and let them "rain" down as your toddler tries to catch them.
    - Sing: "Apples fallin' down, won't you try and catch some.
      Apples fallin' down, won't you try and catch some.
      Apples fallin' down, won't you try and catch some.
      Catch some if you can." (throw apples up in air)
- Fast and Slow game: play music with fast/slow tempos. Provide brightly colored scarf of fabric ribbon and have your child move it to the music

Game Time:
- Pickin' Apples: Crumple red, yellow, and green construction paper up into balls. Put them into a laundry basket and then dump in middle of floor. Have your child pick the "apples" up and put them in the basket. For added fun…just have them do it fast, slow, by crawling, by hopping, by slithering, etc.
- Batter Up! Have child hold empty paper towel tube like a bat. Use crumpled paper for the ball.

Snack Idea:
- Eat applesauce and graham crackers

Fieldtrip Ideas:
- Grocery Store – visit produce section; let child pick apple of each color
- Apple orchard or farm

B
Color: Red
Number: 1
Shape: Circle
Scripture: …The Lord is my helper, and I will not fear… Hebrews 13:6

Theme: **Bears and Camping**

Bible: David and Goliath
- Scripture: …The Lord is my helper, and I will not fear… Hebrews 13:6
- Story: David and Goliath. Keep it simple: God helped David kill a big, mean bear and lion. Then God helped David kill a Giant. Bible Concept: God helps me.
- Have toddler pretend to be giant. Gently toss a balled up piece of paper (stone) at him and have him fall down. Toddlers will want to do this over and over.
- Set up a "camp" at the Building Center today. Provide sleeping bag and flashlight. Remind children that God is our helper. We should not be afraid.

Theme Learning:
- Talk about what you would need to take if you went camping…backpack, sleeping bag, cooking pan, flashlights, fishing pole, etc.
- Discuss where you might camp…state park, mountains, woods, backyard, etc. Show brochures showing some great campground sites.
- Discuss what you might do while you are camping…fishing, telling campfire stories, cooking over the campfire, etc.
- Discuss what kinds of wildlife and plants you might see if you went camping…bears, deer, rabbits, birds…variety of trees such as oak and pine…watch out for poison ivy…

Letter Skills:
- Sound it Out: B says "b" like bubbles
- Play a Game: Blow bubbles and have toddler practice saying "b" as he pops them; make him say "b" to get a turn to blow
- Decorate blank letter B with band-aids
- Use dry beans to make letter B (capital and lower case); you may choose to provide a written B b for students to cover with beans
- Letter B collage-let children find and cut or tear out pictures of things that start with b. Glue to construction paper to make a Letter B collage.

Math:
- "Go Fishing" using toy fishing pole and construction paper fish with gem clip taped on so that the magnet in the fishing pole with stick on; count fish as you pull them up
- Pour sand into a shallow dish or baking pan (or use rice). Have toddler practice writing number 1 with finger in the sand.

- Bean counters-Write the numbers 1-5 on small paper cups; students should put 1 bean in the cup labeled 1, 2 beans in the cup labeled 2, etc. If you have several bean varieties, the students may sort the beans.

Shape Practice:
- Bubble Wrap: Look around the house for bubble wrap that may have come in a package lying around or ask a mailing service store to donate a small piece to you; show toddler that bubble wrap is made up of tiny circles filled with air; toddlers love popping bubble wrap by stomping on it...sometimes it is too tough for them to pop with fingers
- Circle Bear Project: Use brown construction paper to cut out various sized circles and have toddler glue together to make a bear. Large circle for face; two small circles for ears; really large circle for body; four small circles for legs; draw on face with marker

Color: Red
- Paint Red Campfire: Google campfire coloring sheet and print out; have toddler finger paint with red on the campfire (older toddlers can use brush or Q-tip to paint with)

Art:
- Bubble Painting: Fill empty yogurt container with dish detergent, acrylic paint and a little water; mix well and use old bubble wand to blow bubbles on white paper; try using several yogurt containers for multicolored bubble painting (note: cover area with newspaper or do outside)

- Bouncy Ball Art: Buy roll of wrapping paper from $1 Store. Go outside and unroll wrapping paper, turn upside down so that white side is up and lay across sidewalk. Put several colors of paint into paper plates. Roll balls into paint and have toddler drop onto the white side of the wrapping paper. The balls will bounce around making a beautiful bouncy ball art piece. (messy, but so fun for a toddler)

- Have toddler color on a brown paper sack; use the sack for trail mix made below in Snack Idea section

Story Time:
- Bears in the Night by Jan and Stan Berenstain (or any Berenstain Bears' book)
- Brown Bear, Brown Bear, What Do You See? by Eric Carle
- We're Going on a Bear Hunt by Michael Rosen
- The Three Bears -Little Golden Book (or any version of this story)

Music:
- Bean Shaker: Make a shaker using an empty Pringles can filled with beans and duct taped closed. Use colorful drawer/shelf liner to decorate the can or use a piece of the wrapping paper used in the Art project above. Play music from CD or radio and have your toddler shake away!
- Dr. Jean Sings Silly Songs CD has a great, interactive "Going on a Bear Hunt" song that toddlers love! (can find online or at Teacher Supply store)
- Sing as your toddler acts out:
   Teddy Bear, Teddy Bear, turn around.
   Teddy Bear, Teddy Bear touch the ground.
   Teddy Bear, Teddy Bear climb the stairs.
   Teddy Bear, Teddy Bear say your prayers.
   Teddy Bear, Teddy Bear, turn out the light.
   Teddy Bear, Teddy Bear, say "Goodnight."

Game Time:
- Sit on floor with toddler and roll ball back and forth. Toddlers love this simple, repetitive game. They usually aren't able to catch a ball yet, but love rolling one. Play music and whomever has the ball when the music stops, must name something that starts with B
- Beanbag Toss: toss beanbags into a laundry basket; you can make beanbags by simply filling the bottom of old tube socks with rice or beans and tying securely.

Snack Idea:
- Serve mini-marshmallows and hotdog cut with Toddler Bites Hotdog Cutter for a "camp-out snack." (Choking Alert-be sure child eats marshmallows one by one and be sure the hot dog is split lengthwise and then cut into ½ inch pieces)
- Trail Mix-make toddler friendly trail mix using mini-marshmallows, plain M&M's, pretzel sticks, and dry cereal
- Serve Teddy Grahams or Gummy Bears

Fieldtrip Ideas:
- Take a camping trip outside on your center's playground. Set up a tent and quilts to sit on. Have lunch outside as well. Be sure to have children each bring their favorite teddy bear.
- Visit a state park
- Have Smokey Bear (local Forestry Department) visit and talk about properly putting out camp fires.

C
Color: Red
Number: 1
Shape: Circle
Scripture: …Whoso trusteth in the Lord, happy is he. Proverbs 16:20

Theme: **Clowns/Circus**

Bible:
- Scripture: …Whoso trusteth in the Lord, happy is he. Proverbs 16:20
- Tell story of Daniel in the Lion's Den. Keep it simple: Daniel loved God and prayed to Him. Some men tricked the King into making it law that people could not pray to God. Daniel prayed anyway. The King had to throw Daniel into a lion's den for punishment. God sent an angel to shut the lion's mouths. The King saw what happened and said that everyone should pray to God.
- Make paper plate lion stick puppet-glue yarn around edge of small paper plate for mane; draw on face; tape Popsicle stick on back

Theme Learning:
- What people might you see at a circus? ringmaster, clowns, lion tamer, juggler, tightrope walkers, acrobats, magicians, cannon shooters, etc.
- What animals might you see at a circus? elephants, bears, lion, horses, dogs, etc.
- What things might be happening at a circus? someone selling popcorn, peanuts, etc., jugglers juggling, acrobats swinging on the trapeze, animals performing, etc.
- What does it take to get ready for a circus? choosing an act, making the costumes, decorating, sending invitations or selling tickets, face painting, making props, practicing and have a dress rehearsal

Letter Skills:
- Sound it Out-C says "c" like a clown.
- Play a Game: Draw or print out a picture of a clown. If child says "c" sound, he may add a spot to the clown's shirt. Hang decorated clown on the refrigerator or on child's door.
- Decorate blank C by gluing on cotton balls
- Shape a pipe cleaner to look like letter C. Glue to construction paper. Cut pipe cleaner in half and make little c. Glue beside the big C.

Math
- Put shaving cream (not gel kind) onto kitchen table. Spread the shaving cream out and have toddler practice writing number 1. Then just let toddler have fun! It won't hurt the table, but instead will make it shine and smell so clean! This activity is messy, but will be a sure favorite for your toddler. You could always use whipped cream if you afraid your toddler may put the shaving cream in his mouth.

- Purchase animal crackers to use as Math manipulates. Count the animals…sort the animals, etc.

Shape Practice
- Potato Stamping: Print out coloring page of a clown (Google for one). Use a potato cut in half and paper plates with various colors of paint to do circle stamping all around the picture to represent "juggling balls." Of course this could be done simply on plain paper as well. The potatoes are easy for little hands to handle.
- Circle Stamping-dip open end of paper cup or empty toilet roll into paint and stamp lots of circles

Color
- Use face paint or a non toxic marker to "paint" your child's nose red like a clown. Pass around a safe mirror and let students see their red clown noses.
- Play "I Spy." Look for things that are red. You may choose for children to go and get the item and put it into a laundry basket for the children to explore during Center Time.

Art
- Homemade crayons. C is for crayons. Peel paper from old, broken crayons and break into small pieces. Fill mini muffin tin with small pieces. Put into oven at 200 degrees for about 10 minutes or until crayons melt. Let cool (I put them in the freezer for about 10 minutes to speed this along). These homemade crayons are the perfect size for little toddler hands. Provide white paper and let your toddlers color away! Display artwork. Store crayons in Ziploc bags.
- Draw a simple circus tent outline. Have children count out 1 of each type of animal from a bag of animal crackers and glue inside the tent…1 giraff, 1 elephant, 1 horse, etc.
- Handprint elephant-paint child's hand with gray paint and have him press onto white paper; when dry add eye, ear and tail

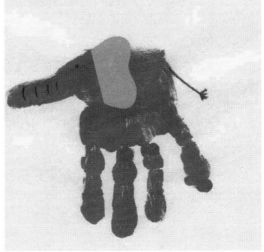

Story Time:
- <u>Clifford at the Circus</u> by Norman Bridwell
- <u>If I Ran the Circus</u> by Dr. Seuss
- <u>Spot Goes to the Circus</u> by Eric Hill
- <u>Curious George Goes to the Circus</u> by Margaret Rey

Music
- Play music and have the children move like a circus animal: elephant, tiger, bear, horse, etc.
- Make homemade drum and have child do circus drum rolls. Drum can be as simple as pots with two wooden spoons. It's loud, but toddlers LOVE it!
- Sing: "If You're Happy and You Know It."

Game Time
- Balloon Toss: SUPERVISE WELL. Blow up several balloons and tie. Have toddlers try to keep balloons up in the air. Don't let them touch the floor. Fun!
- Circus Train: tie 3 laundry baskets together with yarn to make a train; add a rope handle to the first basket; let child give stuffed animals a "train ride"
- Tight Rope Walking-place a jump rope on the ground and let children try to walk along the "tightrope."
- Elephant, Elephant, Lion (like Duck, Duck, Goose)
- Jumping Through Hoops-children must take turns jumping through a hoola-hoop
- Pin the Nose on the Clown..use red balloons blown up slightly for the nose; affix with masking tape.

Snack Idea
- Eat animal crackers.
- Buy a bag of cotton candy sold at most snack bars is larger Super Center stores. What a treat!
- Serve hotdogs (a circus favorite) cut using Toddler Bites Hotdog Cutter. Squirt red ketchup and discuss the color red.
- Ice Cream Clowns-give each child a scoop of ice cream and have them put a cone shaped ice cream cone on top. Decorate the clown's face with candy and enjoy!

Fieldtrip Ideas:
- Watch the movie, "Dumbo."
- Invite a balloon artist or clown to come to class
- Fall is the time when the circus usually comes to town. Check your local paper, you may get lucky and find a real circus to attend!

D
Color: Red
Number: 1
Shape: Circle
Scripture: To everything there is a season…a time to plant, and a time to pluck up
that which is planted… Ecclesiastes 3:1-2

Theme: **Down on the Farm**

Bible:
- Scripture: To everything there is a season…a time to plant, and a time to pluck up that which is planted… Ecclesiastes 3:1-2
- Tell story of the Sower. Keep it simple: A farmer went out to plant seeds. Some seeds fell on the hard ground and the birds ate them. Some seeds fell on the rocks and didn't grow strong roots and dried up in the hot sun. Some seeds fell in the weeds, but the weeds shaded the sunlight and they couldn't grow. Some fell in good soil and grew nice vegetables. We should be like the seed that grew and listen and learn more about God.
- Role-play the story. Go outside and plant vegetables in a small corner of your backyard or in large pots. Tomatoes grow well in pots. You could just plant flower seeds in a pot if you'd rather.

Theme Learning:
- Discuss what you might find on a farm: animals (kinds), farmer/family, tractors, garden (vegetables)
- Discuss Gardens (See Music section for vegetable review game/song)
- Discuss the work the farmer and his family does: feed animals, tend the garden, build/repair fences, collect milk and eggs, sell produce to market, etc.
- Discuss animals found on the farm and their uses: cows/milk, chickens/eggs, sheep/ wool, horse/ride, goats/clearing tall grass, etc.

Letter Skills: D
- Sound It Out: D says "d" like dog.
- Decorate blank letter D to look like a Dalmatian by using Q-tips to paint black spots inside the outline of letter D.
- Letter D Box-use an empty wet wipes box labeled with letter D, d; add things that start with D and discuss. (dime, dollar, toy donut, small stuffed dog, etc.)
- Feed the Pig-Use print pig cutout provided and mount onto half of a file folder; cut hole for mouth and provide yellow squares cut from construction paper for corn; have child "feed" the pig each time he can tell you what letter D says when asked; use flashcards to review other letter-child may feed the pig each time correct.
- Letter F Hunt-give each child a magazine page and let him/her hunt for and highlight or circle all the f's they find
- Playdough-form letter F,f...also provide F cookie cutter as well as the other letters you have already covered this year (A-E)

Math:

- Bury toy bones (or use empty toilet rolls for bones) in the sandbox and have toddler dig them up; count how many he finds
- Use chocolate pudding (piggy mud) on paper plate to make #1's with finger
- Haystack Counting-place raffia or straw inside Styrofoam cup; have child place one plastic fork (pitch fork) into straw; write number 1 on cup; take pitchfork in and out of straw as he counts number 1 (for enrichment, make cups for other numbers and provide enough plastic forks to stick in correct cups)

Shape Practice:

- Circle Mobile: Collect old CD's (post office usually has a stack of free AOL Internet demo CD's laying on the counter. Attach string to a few of these and tie to a clothes hanger so that they hang down. The mirrored CD's reflect the light and make nice rainbow effect when hung from a ceiling fan pull. Refer to shape of CD's (circles) to reinforce the shape this month.
- Shape Tracing: Collect the lids from various household items in your cabinet or refrigerator. For example: canister tops, oatmeal container lids, coffee can top, etc. Give your toddlers paper and a marker and let them try to trace around the tops to make circles. Toddlers will need help holding the tops down and guiding the marker around until they get the hang of it.

Color:

- Egg Color Match Up: Wash empty egg carton. Use marker to color the inside bottom of each egg cup with different color. Use plastic eggs in those same colors and let your toddler place matching plastic egg in correct egg cup.

Art:

- Mud Painting: Cut pig shape from pink construction paper. Let your child paint with brown paint or for even more fun paint with chocolate pudding (mud!)
- Sticker Farm Scene: Toddlers LOVE stickers and will usually work intently. Purchase farm animal stickers in the card and stationary area at larger stores. Let them add the stickers to a piece of green construction paper or a farm coloring sheet for a farm scene.
- Tractor track painting: Put black paint on a paper plate and let your toddler roll the tractor in the paint and across white paper to make tractor tracks.
- Pig Nose: Cut one egg cup from a cardboard egg carton and let your child paint it pink. Draw on two oval nose holes and attach elastic (or yarn) to each side of the egg cup for a piggy nose! Provide mirror so your child can see that he's a pig!
- Cotton ball Sheep: Print out sheep coloring page. Have toddler glue on cotton balls.

Story Time:

- The Little Red Hen (Little Golden Book or any variation)
- The Big Red Barn by Margaret Wise Brown
- Rooster's Off to See the World by Eric Carle
- If You Give a Pig a Pancake by Laura Numeroff

Music:
- Sing "Old McDonald Had a Farm" Go through all the animals sounds this week, but also include farm machinery sounds. For example: the tractor on the farm goes "brrr" brrr" "brrr"
- Felt Veggies-Cut out vegetable shapes from felt or fun foam (about 33 cent per piece at large retail store in craft department). "Plant" vegetables around floor like a garden. Give your child a basket and let him pick the veggies as you sing, "Where oh where is Farmer ____? Where oh where is Farmer ____? Where oh where is Farmer ____? Way down yonder in the veggie patch. Pickin' up tomatoes, puttin' them in his basket; pickin' up corn, puttin' it in his basket; pickin' up carrots, putting them in his basket. Way down yonder in the veggie patch." Let him try to identify and find the correct veggie you call out.
- Sing-The Animals on the Farm Go…(tune of the Wheels on the Bus); use different animals/sounds

Game Time:
- Pin the Tail on the Piggy: Use pink pipe cleaner tail.
- Play "Doggy, Doggy, Where's Your Bone" by hiding toy bone and having toddler find it.
- Feed the Pig-Get a manila folder and open it like upside down V so that it can stand alone. Find or draw picture of a pig face. (Google it) Glue the pig onto one side of folder and cut opening for mouth of pig. Stand folder back up like upside down V. Cut out lots of yellow construction paper squares (corn). Let your child "fed the pig" by putting the squares of "corn" into it's mouth.
- Milk the Cow: Fill a rubber glove with water and tie it like a balloon. Let your toddler grab the fingers and pretend they are cow utters. Let him milk the cow. For added fun, use a straight pin to make holes in the tips of the gloves fingers so that as your child "milk" the water will actually come out.

Snack Idea
- Dog bone biscuits: pinch the middle of canned biscuits together to form bone shape and bake
- Milk Shake
- Homemade butter: Fill a clean, empty baby food jar halfway with whipping cream. Put the lid on tight and let your toddler shake away! The whipping cream will turn to butter! Spread on crackers or a piece of bread for a yummy snack! If you are worried about the jar breaking, try a clean, plastic peanut butter jar...takes more shaking, but makes more butter!

Fieldtrip Ideas:
- Visit a local farm
- Visit a local farmers market and talk about the many vegetables found there
- Visit the produce section of a grocery store; explain that farmers grow the vegetables and fruits found there

E
Color: Orange
Number: 2
Shape: Square
Scripture: If any of you lack wisdom, let him ask of God…and it shall be given him.
James 1:5

Theme: **Emotions/Feelings**

Bible

- Scripture: If any of you lack wisdom, let him ask of God…and it shall be given him. James 1:5
- Tell the story of Solomon. Keep it simple: God spoke to Solomon in a dream. He asked Solomon what he would wish for if he could have anything he wanted. Solomon chose wisdom. One day two women came to the king to solve a problem. Both women said that a baby was theirs. Solomon used his wisdom to find out who the real mommy was. He solved the problem.
- Make a "Thinking Cap"-decorate old baseball cap by gluing misc. items on to it; suggestions: jewels, fun foam shapes, feathers, light bulb shaped mini erasers (great idea symbol), etc.

Theme Learning

- What are emotions? List examples: happy, sad, mad, proud, nervous, excited, etc.
- Talk about the most common emotions: happy/sad. Discuss what might cause you to feel this way. In advance, purchase small, white paper plates. Draw a happy face on one side and a sad face on the other side. Tape to a popsicle stick. Give one to each child. Read the following scenarios and tell the children to decide if they would be happy/sad and show that fac.
  Your friend breaks your toy
  You go see a movie
  You skin your knee
  You go to see your grandmother
  You get to eat an ice cream cone

- Show pictures of people showing various emotions (cut from magazines); talk about what emotion they are showing and what might have happened to them to make them feel this way
- Discuss properly reacting to emotions-Ex. when we are mad, we can count to ten to calm down…when we are nervous or scared, we can say a prayer and ask God to be with us…

Letter Skills
- Sound it Out: E says "e" like a little old lady who can't hear well... "Eh, What'd you say sonny? Eh" Toddlers will think this is funny especially if you borrow a pair of "little old lady" glasses and really act out the part!
- Decorate blank letter E using colored egg shells (left over from Easter or color your own using food coloring); looks like a colorful mosaic
- Letter Hunt-give each child a magazine page; have him look for letter E and highlight
- Popsicle Stick Letter E-have students lay one stick flat

Math
- Trace Number 2-cut out number two shape from inexpensive plastic placemat for durability; have child trace around the number 2 using a marker
- Number 2 Rubbing-place 2 pennies under white paper and let child rub crayon over top to reveal two penny impressions; write 1 and 2 beside the pennies (Note: monitor this activity since the pennies present a choking risk)
- Count pairs of objects-unroll a pair of socks; count them; roll them back up and repeat

Shape Practice
- Square Collage-glue square pieces of fabric, magazine clippings, paper sack squares, etc. all over a piece of paper
- Play dough Squares-form squares with play dough by rolling a long "snake" and bending to form 4 equal sides
- Play "I Spy Squares"-have students look around the room and find squares

Color
- Happy Feet Painting-tape a large piece of paper to the sidewalk outside or garage floor. Pour orange paint into a reusable pie pan or paper plate. Have child step into pan and then onto the paper and stomp around happily. The result will be a happy feet painting that he will have so much fun making!
- "I'm so blue," is a term used to mean, "I'm sad." Watch what happens when you mix blue paint with orange...it turns a happy purplish color!
- Cut out orange squares from construction paper. Spread out all across the living room floor. Play happy music as child picks up all the orange squares. Let child glue the squares to another piece of construction paper for a great fine motor skill building activity.

Art
- Feelings Collage-have toddler tear out pages from magazine that show various types of feelings (or do this in advance and just discuss pictures and have toddler glue them onto construction paper)
- Paint with watercolor paint set to happy, peppy music and then to sad, slow music
- Paper plate happy face-give each child a paper plate, add large button eyes and yarn hair and use popcorn for the smile (looks like lots of teeth)

Story Time
- Alexander and the Terrible, No Good, Horrible Day by Judith Viorst
- The Very Lonely Firefly by Eric Carle
- How are you Peeling? by Saxton Freyman and Joost Elffers
- Feelings by Aliki

Music
- Sing: "If You're Happy and You Know it" using these motions (clap your hands, wiggle your fingers, scratch your back, touch your toes, etc)
- Mirror of Emotions: glue yarn "hair" to hand held mirror and have child look into mirror and show various emotions
- Play lively music while you pass a bean bag; when the music stops the child holding the beanbag must go and find someone and do whatever it takes to make them smile
- Play music and have the children stomp around as if angry, skip around as if happy, mope around as if sad, jump around as if excited, Stop the music between emotions.

Game Time
- Happy/Sad sorting: In advance cut out magazine photos showing people who are happy or sad. Take two large brown grocery sacks and draw a happy face on one and a sad face on the other. Open the bags and place side by side. Have toddler look at picture and drop magazine photos into the correct bag
- Use toy or old phone to call each child. Ask questions like, "What is your name? What makes you happy? What does your mouth do when you are happy? What do you like to eat? What do like to play with?…"

Snack Idea
- Rice cake smiley face-spread rice cake with peanut butter (or vanilla frosting if you have a child with a peanut allergy); add raisin eyes, M&M nose, and mini chocolate chips for the smile

Other
- Discuss different types of Feelings: Happy, Sad, Mad, Scared, Excited
- Have toddler show the different emotions with his face
- Provide safe mirror for child to look at throughout the week; when you see him showing an emotion get the mirror and have him try to describe what emotion he is showing

Fieldtrip Ideas
- If you have a Brewster's Ice Cream shop around, visit it this week. Your toddler will receive a free sample ice cream cone with sprinkles for hair and little candy eyes (happy face ice cream cone that will make your toddle very happy); You can always make your own version of this happy face snack

F

Color: Orange

Number: 2

Shape: Square

Scripture: …Blessed are they that hear the word of God, and keep it. Luke 11:28

Theme: **Fish**

Bible

- Scripture: …Blessed are they that hear the word of God, and keep it. Luke 11:28
- Tell the story of Jonah and the Big Fish. Keep it simple: God told Jonah to go to Nineveh. Jonah did not obey. He got on a ship and sailed the other way. A storm came. Jonah told the sailors to throw him overboard. They did, and the storm went away. God sent a big fish to swallow Jonah. Jonah told God he was sorry for not obeying. The big fish spit Jonah out. Jonah went to Nineveh and obeyed God.
- Have toddler decorate a brown lunch sack using markers or crayons. When finished, stuff with newspaper. Have him place a small toy person inside (or cut one from magazine and mount on cereal box cardboard for durability). Twist the open end and fan out (like fish tale). Use to re-tell story.

Theme Learning

- Where do fish live? Ponds, lakes, rivers, streams, oceans, fish tanks
- What kinds of fish would be found in ponds, lakes and rivers? (show pictures) catfish, bass, brim, etc.
- What kinds of fish would be found in oceans? (show pictures) Discuss salt water fish and how they differ from the fish found in ponds, lakes and rivers. Sharks, dolphins, whales, clown fish, etc.
- What kinds of fish do people keep as pets? What do these pets need? Water, food, tank with filter and possibly light

Letter Skills

- Sound it Out: F says "f" like fish
- Play a game: Construct fishing pole using stick, yarn, and magnet on end. Make fish cutouts in various bright colors; add metal brad for eye. If your child can say "f" sound, let him catch a fish.
- Decorate blank letter F using fingerprints
- Letter F Hunt-give each child a magazine page and let him highlight or circle all the letter F's he can find.
- F Collage-look in magazines for pictures of things that start with the "f" sound

Numbers
- Use the fishing pole and fish from Letter Skills activity above. Have your toddler fish and give you the fish that he catches. Count them together.
- Help toddler sort the fish into colors (put all orange together, yellow together, etc.)
- Cut out various sized fish and have toddler put them in order from smallest to biggest.
- 2 fish in a Ziploc fish bowl-cut out a fish bowl shape from construction paper; cut out the center so there is an opening; staple a Ziploc bag to the back; have student put green Easter grass (sea weed), a sea shell and 2 fun foam fish to the bag, zip the bag closed and staple
- Beach Towel Counting-spread a beach towel in the middle of the circle; lay lots of shells on the towel and let children take turns putting them in group of 2

Shape Practice
- Square play area: make a square on the floor using masking tape Try the following activities: have toddler walk around edges of square, jump in and out of square, bring stuffed animals into the square and pretend it's a boat, etc.
- Square stamping: Take any wooden block or other object that is shaped like a square; dip one end in paint and have toddler do square stamping on paper
- "I Spy" Orange Squares-tape orange squares to the wall at various spots where the children can easily see while seated at the carpet; call on students to look around and find an orange square and go and get it.

Color
- Paint a goldfish: use paper plate to make cutting tail shape from paper plate and gluing the tale to another round paper plate. Let your child paint this with orange paint. Hang in bathroom from shower curtain rod.
- Make an orange crayon holder: Have child paint a clean, empty soup using orange paint. When dry, use it to store crayons.
- Seashell impressions-have children press sea shells into orange balls of play dough and let dry; these make really nice seashell fossils; if you'd like give each child a small ball of red and a small ball of white play dough and instruct them to kneed it with their fingers and watch as it turns into orange

Art

- Decorate Shower Curtain: purchase a blue shower curtain at your local $1 Store; Let your child use a fish shaped stamp (found in craft department of large retail stores) to dip in paint and press onto shower curtain. You can "clean up" any messy painting by adding green seaweed squiggly accents and blue bubbles in the water. Display on one wall in your room for an instant underwater aquarium.
- Fish Bowl: Cut top part off of white paper plate to make a fish bowl; have toddler paint blue using finger paint or paintbrush (older toddler); add fish stickers or cutouts when dry

Music:
- Sing "Row, Row, Row Your Boat" while sitting in large square "boat" from Shape activity above.
- Fish Pokey: sung like Hokey Pokey, but you put your fins, gills, tail, etc. in

Game Time
- Fly Swatter Bubbles: Fly swatters make great bubble wands and produce hundreds of tiny bubbles each time; Use pie pan to pour bubble solution in and dip with fly swatter
- Beach Ball fun: play with beach balls
- Dive under the Ocean-place pictures of fish on the floor; have each child hold the edge of a large blue sheet; pick up the sheet and shake gently like the ocean waves; call different children to "dive" under and bring up a fish
- Fish, Fish, Shark-played like Duck, Duck, Goose

Snack Ideas
- Place goldfish crackers in small cups; use pretzels with ends dipped in peanut butter to snag the fish
- Make blue jell-o and add gummy fish
- Make and serve sea shell shaped macaroni and cheese

**Toddlers LOVE to watch fish swim; purchase an inexpensive aquarium to put in corner of your bathroom sink (this would really add to the ocean theme bathroom from the Art activity idea above); Colorful Beta fish are a great choice! You will be surprised at how often your toddler returns to the bathroom to check on his new pet!

Fieldtrip Ideas
- Visit Aquarium if you live near one…i.e. Atlanta, Chattanooga…
- Watch movie, "Nemo"

G

Color: Orange
Number: 2
Shape: Square
Scripture: Casting all your care upon Him; for He careth for you.
1 Peter 5:7

Theme: **Mother Goose Rhymes**

Bible
- Scripture: Casting all your care upon Him; for He careth for you. 1 Peter 5:7
- Tell Story of The Lost Sheep. Keep it simple: Jesus told a story about a man who was taking care of sheep. One sheep went off and got lost. The man left all his other sheep to go and find the one sheep. He really cared for that one sheep even though he still had lots more sheep. God cares for each of us just that much! Bible Concept: God cares for us.
- Use the lamb made in Art to act out the story. Hide the lamb and let a child go and find it.

Theme Learning
- Introduce Nursery Rhymes. Who was Mother Goose? Fairy tales and rhymes from many authors collected together under the Mother Goose name
- Humpty Dumpty-read and then re-tell the story using simple stick puppets or props (plastic egg, toy horse, etc.)
- Little Bo Peep-read and play Shepherd, Shepherd Where's Your Sheep game (see Game Time)
- The Old Woman in the Shoe-read and act out
- Name that rhyme review game-describe a rhyme (such as characters or action) and see if children can guess which nursery rhyme you are speaking of

Letter Skills
- G says "g" like gum
- Play a Game: Say G says "g" like gum and pretend to chew gum
- Feed the monster-draw a monster on poster board and cut out the opening for the mouth; if child can say "g" sound properly when asked, "What does g say?" he may feed the monster a piece of gum (paper sleeve around stick gum like Juicy Fruit) *You can use this poster for reviewing lots of skills throughout the year
- Decorate blank G with glitter; let your child use a small paint brush to brush on the paint before you shake the glitter onto letter G
- Letter G Hunt-give each child a sheet from a magazine and have him circle or highlight the letter G's
- Playdough G's-roll playdough like a snake and then curve around to form G,g

Math

- Mitten Lacing: Cut a mitten shape from cereal box cardboard. Punch holes around the edges. Have your toddler lace thread all around the mitten. Note: Be sure to tape the end of the yarn so that it won't fray. You could also use a shoelace, which works very well. (The Three Little Kittens)
- Egg Carton Counting: Use an empty egg carton and old plastic Easter eggs to practice counting. Discuss what a dozen is. (Humpty Dumpty)
- Graph Favorite Mother Goose Rhyme-create a simple graph and include several of the rhymes you've discussed this week; go around the circle and let each child tell you which is their favorite; color one square for each child's choice; count to see which is most/least favorite
- Roll the dice-have students take turns rolling the dice to see if they land on 2; those large foam dice are great, but any size will work as long as the children know that they should remain seated and let the roller retrieve the dice and pass to the next person

Shape Practice

- Square Wall: use square shaped couch pillow as Humpty Dumpty's wall; roll play the rhyme as your toddler "falls" from wall (lays back on floor); try to "put him back together" by sitting him back up on the pillow.

Color

- Egg Mosaic: Hard boil half a dozen eggs and use food coloring to color them orange. Peel eggs and crush eggshells into pieces. Let toddler glue pieces to goldfish shape.
- Make orange: Give your child paper cup or paper bowl and squeeze in red and white paint. Have him use Popsicle stick to stir paint until it turns orange! He will be amazed. Let him use a paintbrush or Q-tip to paint an orange pumpkin. (Google for a pumpkin coloring page) As child works, you could recite rhyme, "Peter, Peter, Pumpkin Eater."

Art

- Toilet Roll Candlestick: Take a cardboard toilet roll and stuff with red and or orange tissue paper so that some of the tissue paper is sticking up from the top like the flame on a candle. Let your child color or use stickers to decorate their candle.
- Handprint Sheep: Trace your child's hand on black construction paper; have him glue cotton balls on palm part of handprint. The tips of four fingers are legs; the thumb is the head.
- Old Woman Who Lived in the Shoe Collage: Cut out a shoe shape from paper (or Google this theme and find a coloring page of Shoe); help your toddler find and tear out pictures from magazines of different children and glue onto shoe

Story Time

- Read book: James Marshall's Mother Goose by James Marshall
- Read book: Bad Egg: The True Story of Humpty Dumpty by Sarah Hayes

- Read book: Sylvia Long's Mother Goose by Sylvia Long
- Read book: The Real Mother Goose by Blanch Fisher Wright

Music
- Hey Diddle Diddle: Sing this nursery rhyme and have toddler run around with plastic plate when you get to that part in the song.
- Twinkle, Twinkle, Little Star: Tape a yellow star cutout to a straw. Decorate with glitter if you'd like. Have your child hold the star wand and sing, "Twinkle, Twinkle, Little Star…" Have him hold it up when you sing, "Up Above the World So High…"
- Sing, "Mary Had a Little Lamb"

Game Time
- Jack Be Nimble: Use the candlestick made in Art; place it on the floor and have toddler jump over it as you recite the nursery rhyme Jack Be Nimble. Substitute your child's name, "___ Be Nimble, ___ Be Quick! ___ Jump Over the Candlestick!"
- Shepherd, Shepherd Where's Your Sheep Game: Have one child be "the shepherd;" have him close eyes while you give the sheep to one child to hide in his lap or behind his back; Sing, "Shepherd, Shepherd, Where's Your Sheep? It ran away while you were asleep!" Let him have three guesses to figure out who found the sheep.

Snack Idea
- Eggs: Cut up and eat hardboiled eggs from Art activity above.
- Candle Cupcake: Toddler LOVE blowing out candles! Use birthday candle on cupcake and let your child blow it out
- Muffin Man Muffins: Make muffins and pretend to be "The Muffin Man" as you plate them (purchase several premixed packages that just need water added…one for each group; have kids help dump mix, add water, take turns stirring, and fill muffin cups using small ¼ cup dry measuring cup)
- Pat a Cake Biscuits-serve with jam

Fieldtrip Ideas
- Visit your local library and ask the Children's Librarian to read some Mother Goose stories to the children

Special Holiday Week
Letter: Review
Color: Orange
Number: Review
Shape: Square
Scripture: Create in me a clean heart, O God; and renew a right spirit within me.
Psalm 51:10

Theme: **Halloween Week (Christian Version)**

Bible
- Scripture: Create in me a clean heart, O God; and renew a right spirit within me. Psalm 51:10
- Tell story of the Christian Pumpkin. Keep it simple: (Use real pumpkin to illustrate if possible) We are like this pumpkin. God picks us up and washes us clean (forgives our sin); He then helps get us get rid of all the bad things we do and replace them with good things (scoop out insides)…He helps us remember to look at good things and use our mouth to speak kind words (carve face); He puts his light inside so that we can shine that light as we tell others about Him (put tea candle inside and light).

Theme Learning
- Read the book, <u>From Seed to Pumpkin</u> by Wendy Pfeffer (order on Amazon if you cannot find in your local library)
- Pumpkin uses: pumpkin pie, carving, roasted pumpkin seeds, decorations
- What's in a pumpkin?
- Taste Test – open a can of pumpkin like you would use to make pumpkin pie; give each child a plastic spoon with a little pumpkin on it; describe the smell and taste; graph how many children like versus dislike the taste of pumpkin

Letter Skills
- Review Letters covered so far
- Review all letter boxes A – G (each week, fill empty wet wipes containers with things that begin with the letter of the week…you will have 26 boxes at the end of the year)
- Sing the Alphabet Song to review all letters
- Erase the letter – write letters learned so far on the board (A-G); have student come up and erase the letter you say; repeat so that everyone has a turn
- Pick a Pocket game – purchase one of those hanging shoe organizers with lots of pockets; put a letter in each (cut out from paper or use ABC magnets); children take turns coming up and pulling letter from pocket – he should tell what letter it is and what sound it makes
- Trace magnetic alphabet letters
- Alphabet stamping – purchase a set of ABC stamps and stamp pad and let the children stamp the letters on white paper

- Play dough with alphabet cookie cutters
- Sing: What's the Sound song to review all letters
  <u>What's the Sound</u> – tune B-I-N-G-O
  What's the sound that starts these words
  _____ and _____ and _____
  / / is the sound, / / is the sound, / / is the sound
  That starts ____, _____, and _____.

Math

- Review Numbers covered so far
- Pumpkin Patch Counting – cut out pumpkin shapes from orange construction paper; call out a number and have volunteer put that many pumpkins in the "pumpkin patch" (middle of Circle); repeat with other numbers
- Flashlight Writing – turn off the lights and use a flashlight to "write" a number on the wall or ceiling; children must try to guess what number you wrote
- Who Has # __? game – give each child an index card that has a number on it; call out a number and those children who have it should stand; repeat several times and then let the children switch numbers with their neighbor

Shape Practice

- Shape Sorting: cut out several circles and squares. Place 2 bowls in front of your child. Show him how to put circles in one bowl and squares in the other.
- Place several shoeboxes on a table. Fill them with different colored construction paper pumpkins cut into a variety of sizes. Have your child sort the squares according to size.

Color

- Play with orange play dough – let children mix red with yellow
- Finger paint with orange paint; cut into pumpkin shape when dry; next…glue on yellow yarn and several pumpkin seeds to show what it looks like inside a pumpkin (see Art)
- Show an orange – cut open and look inside; it's orange on the inside and out; stamp with it
- Play I Spy to review colors
- Stand up if you Have on ___ color game – call out a color and have all children with that color on stand

Art

- Halloween Treat Bucket: Ask a local restaurant or school lunchroom to save a large vegetable can for you. Wash the can out and spray paint black. Drill two holes on either side of the can. Let your child decorate with stripes using strips of colorful reflective tape or try glow in the dark paints (found in paint department). Add red ribbon through the drilled holes to make a handle. Take if you go "trunk or treating" at church.

- Decorate mini pumpkins – purchase from Farmer's Market or grocery store; if you are going to visit a pumpkin patch on a fieldtrip, the kids could pick their own at that time
- Finger paint with orange paint (see Color); cut into pumpkin shape when dry; next…glue on yellow yarn and several pumpkin seeds to show what it looks like inside a pumpkin

Music
- Colorful Shaker: Fill an empty water bottle with colorful aquarium rocks; replace lid and duct tape closed. The bottle top is perfect for little toddler sized hands to shake!
- "Alphabats" song – review the letter sounds by singing this song like the old Batman theme song – For example, for letter B sing, "B-B-B-B-B-B-B-B….B-B-B-B-B-B-B-B….Batman!" For letter C, it would be Catman….D would be Datman, etc.

Game Time
- Pumpkin Patch Picking: cut pumpkin shapes from construction paper. Hide around the house and let child find and put into store bought pumpkin trick or treat bucket.
- Drop the Rock: provide large coffee can and have child stand beside can and try to drop the rock into the bucket. He/she will enjoy hearing the loud sound it makes.
- Ring the Bucket: purchase pumpkin Halloween buckets (like children go trick-or-treating with) and ping pong balls; have children take turns trying to toss the ping pong balls into the buckets; count how many go in

Snack Idea
- Pumpkin Tortilla - cut Jack-O-Lantern face into one flour tortilla for each child; place another tortilla (not cut) on paper plate; let child top with grated cheddar cheese; place tortilla with face out on top; put in microwave for about 8 seconds to melt cheese.
- Orange Pumpkin Shaped Jell-O Jigglers

Fieldtrip Ideas
- Visit a pumpkin patch
- Carve pumpkin together – give everyone a chance to scoop out the insides; discuss what the class wants the face to look like; count the seeds
- Have a Fall Festival – set up games such as Pick Up Ducks and Bean Bag Toss and allow children to win prizes

Christian Treat Alternatives
- Candy Corn Christian-fill snack size sandwich bag with candy corn and attach tag that says: *Candy is good and sweet, But knowing Jesus is a real treat! John 3:16*

- Bear Fruit Jelly Beans-fill baggie with fruit flavored jelly beans and attach tag that says, "Bear much fruit." *John 15:8 This is to my Father's glory, that you bear much fruit, showing yourselves to be my disciples.*
- Lifesavers-attach note that says, "Let Jesus be your Life Saver!" *John 14:6 Jesus said to him, "I am the way, the truth, and the life. No one comes to the Father except through Me.*
- Milky Way Creation Candy-tape snack size Milky Way candy bars to index card that says, "God created the Milky Way!" *Genesis 1:1 In the beginning God created the heavens and the earth.*
- Sin Eraser-purchase mini eraser and tape to index card printed with, "God can erase your sin!" *Romans 3:23-24 For all have sinned and fall short of the glory of God, being justified freely by His grace through the redemption that is in Christ Jesus.*
- Hershey's Kisses-fill baggie with kisses and attach note that reads, "God Loves You!" *John 3:16*
- Chocolate Coin Giving-"Give Your All!" *Luke 21: 3 So He said, "Truly I say to you that this poor widow has put in more than all."*

H
Color: Yellow
Number: 3
Shape: Rectangle
Scripture: …By love serve one another. Galatians 5:13

Theme: **Community <u>H</u>elpers**

Bible
- Scripture: …By love serve one another. Galatians 5:13
- Story: Jesus Feeds 5000. Keep it simple: Many people loved to hear Jesus speak. A big crowd came and stayed past mealtime. The people were hungry. A boy shared his lunch. He gave Jesus his lunch of 5 loaves of bread and 2 fish. Jesus did something amazing! He broke the bread and fish and it fed everyone with some left over. The boy shared and Jesus fed all the people.
- Cut a slice of bread into 9 small pieces using Toddler Bites Sandwich cutter; re-enact the Bible Story by passing out the bread squares to the class

Theme Learning
- Who are community helpers? Doctors, firemen, policemen, mail carriers, nurses, dentists, etc.
- Garbage Collector-throw crumpled paper around the circle and discuss what it would be like if no one picked up the trash
- Police Officer – have a police officer come and speak to the class during this time, if available
- Doctor-borrow old x-ray from doctor's office; show stethoscope, tongue depressors, etc. Give each child a colorful band aid to wear to remind them of how helpful doctors are

Letter Skills
- Sound it Out: H says "h" like hat
- Play a Game: Collect old hats and caps from closet/attic or borrow some from grandparents; toddler must say "h" sound in order to get to try on a hat
- Decorate blank letter H with happy face or heart stickers
- Hammer H's – in advance write upper and lower case H's all over a piece of white copy paper; make copies for each child; put paper on a piece of thick foam; give student a toy plastic hammer and a wooden golf pin and let him hammer a hole into each letter H
- Happy Face Sticker-student must say "h" sound when asked to receive a Happy Face Sticker

Math
- Write It: Barber Shop Writing-squeeze blue gel shaving crème into large zip lock bag; press air out and seal; spread gel out and let toddler use finger to make number 3

- Police Man Fingerprint Counting-trace child's hand on white paper; have child use ink pad to make fingerprints at tip of each finger; count the fingerprints together…count child's fingers
- Fire Truck Wheel Sorting-use fruit loops for "fire truck wheels" and have toddler sort by color
- Cotton Ball Counting (nurse/doctor)-have toddler pick up 3 cotton balls using tweezers as he counts 1..2..3
- Baker's Blueberry Pancake Counting-make brown construction paper circles for pancakes; draw blue dots for blueberries; make pancakes with 1 blueberry, 2 blueberries, 3 blueberries, etc. Provide plastic spatula for children to pick up blueberry pancake you call out…like the blueberry pancake with 2 blueberries, etc.
- 3's Concept Practice-instruct the students to blink 3 times, clap 3 times, open and close mouth 3 times, pat tummy 3 times, etc.

Shape Practice
- Rectangle hat-cut two pieces of black construction paper rectangles…one large and fat and one thinner for hatband. Have toddler pick biggest/smallest; do this several times before gluing rectangles to form black top hat; attach to front of Burger King crown and you have an instant top hat (Burger King will gladly donate crowns if you just run through the drive through and ask. They have donated enough for entire classes I've taught in the past)
- Rectangle Fire Truck-cut large, red rectangle from construction paper; have toddler add 4 black circles for wheels and decorate with markers
- Rectangle Crackers-provide rectangle shaped crackers for snack today; discuss shape
- How many rectangles can we find? Look around the room and have children call out the rectangles they see…entire ceiling, doors, pictures, etc.

Color
- Play dough Bakery-play with yellow play dough; pretend to make cakes, biscuits, cookies, etc.
- Yellow Menu-Fold yellow construction in half; have toddlers find and glue pictures of food from magazine to make menu; for added learning…look only for foods that are yellow such as bananas, corn, macaroni and cheese, etc.
- Yellow Hunt-Eye Doctors are Community Helpers…pass around a pair of glasses without the frames and let children spot things that are yellow

Art
- Fireman painting-finger paint with red, orange and yellow for a fire picture
- Doctor Collage-Have toddler glue doctor related items to construction paper: Q-tip, cotton ball, band aid, Popsicle stick for tongue depressor
- Toothbrush Painting-use old toothbrush as paintbrush; let child paint on black construction paper cut out like tooth using white paint and toothbrush

- Cards-let toddler help decorate cards for your mailman, your pastor, child's doctor, waitress, etc. Let them give the cards to these people personally
- Fireman Dog-Google dog coloring page or draw on white paper; use Q-tips and black paint to put spots on Dalmatian dog

Story Time
- Community Helpers from A to Z by Bobby Kalman
- Who's Hat is This by Katz Cooper
- Froggy Goes to the Doctor by Jonathan London
- Officer Buckle and Gloria by Peggy Rathmann

Music
- Carpenter--sing "Johnny Works with One Hammer…" use toy hammer to act out song
- Sing, "One Little, Two Little, 3 Little Firemen.." like the Indian song
- Sing and act the toddler favorite, "Patty Cake, Patty Cake, Baker's Man"

Game Time
- Fireman Fun-fill empty squeeze bottle (example: ketchup bottle) with water; let your children take this outside and pretend to be a fireman squirting water from his hose
- Fire Brigade-provide two sand buckets at opposite ends of area; fill one bucket with water and let toddlers dip paper cup into water and take it to other bucket to fill that one up
- "Stop, Drop, and Roll"-toddlers will LOVE role playing these fire drill motions
- Construction Worker-Purchase a pack of golf tees; find large cardboard box; let child use toy hammer to hammer the golf tees into the cardboard box
- Garbage Man-fill empty laundry basket with paper that has been balled up; dump on floor and let toddler be garbage man and pick it up again
- Play "Store": pull out boxes and cans from cupboard; use ironing board that has been raised only to child's height for the checkout counter; provide calculator and store bags; take turns being the cashier and shopper (could put in Dramatic Play area)

Snack Idea
- Build a House-use pieces of bread for house and cut sliced cheese into a triangle for the roof; add rectangle cracker door
- Bake cookies together-let toddlers decorate with sprinkles (Bakery Worker)

Enrichment
- Tour Fire Department
- Mail a letter-let toddler help decorate card/envelope to grandparent; let him add stamp; go to Post Office and let him drop letter into mail slot
- Bake and take cookies to your Pastor; toddler can help decorate the cookies with sprinkles for an extra treat

I
Color: Yellow
Number: 3
Shape: Rectangle
Scripture: If we live in the Spirit, let us also walk in the Spirit. Galatians 5:25

Theme: **Indians**

Bible
- Scripture: If we live in the Spirit, let us also walk in the Spirit. Galatians 5:25
- Tell the story of the Fruits of the Spirit. Keep it simple. Wrap an empty box to look like a beautiful present. Let child open it. When they find nothing is inside, explain that people are sometimes like that. We work on our outsides, but not our insides. Explain that we work on putting these things inside: love, joy, patience, gentleness, peace, faithfulness, goodness, kindness & self-control
- Make a fruit basket to share with elderly friend or neighbor. Let child help pick out fruits from produce section at grocery store. Tell child you are practicing the Fruit of the Spirit: kindness.

Theme Learning
- Indian Alphabet-explain that sometimes Indians used pictures to say things
- Discuss where Indians lived-teepees, homes of wood, homes of mud, etc.
- Discuss what Indian's wore-show fabric samples (leather, fur skins, etc.)
- Discuss what Indians ate-venison, fish, corn, beans, squash, berries, etc.

Letter Skills
- Sound it Out: I says "i" like "itchy dots"
- Play a Game: say "i" sound and add a red, circular price sticker to body; pretend to have "itchy spots"
- Decorate blank I with red "itchy dots" (red price stickers from office supply section of large retail store)
- Add feather to Indian headdress-draw a simple Indian face with headband; cut colorful construction paper feathers; students who can give "I" sound when asked may add a feather to the headdress
- Letter I box-fill empty wet wipes container with small items that start with I such as inches (measuring tape), toy insect, etc.

Math
- Cover #3 with Stickers-use same red, circular stickers from above to make the number 3; write 3 on paper and have toddler put stickers on to cover your writing
- Row your canoe – have students pretend to row a canoe 1 time on the right, 2 times on the left, 3 times on the right, etc.
- Sing-"One Little, Two Little, Three Little Indians" song; hold up fingers as you sing

- Indian Necklace-string noodles onto yarn; be sure to tape end so that it won't fray
  - For colorful noodles, place rubbing alcohol into Ziploc bags and then add food coloring; place noodles in the various baggies and let them sit until they reach the desired color; lay out on paper towels to dry

Shape Practice
- Indian Corn Napkin Rings-cut rectangles from yellow, orange, and brown tissue paper; have toddler ball the rectangles up and glue to toilet roll cut in half; use for Thanksgiving napkin rings

Color
- Yellow play dough Inchworms
- Show a banana-discuss its color
- Feather Painting-use craft feathers as you would paint brushes

Art
- Pillow Case Indian Vest-cut arms holes in side of white or light colored pillow case and cut down the middle in front; have toddler decorate with markers or fabric paint
- Indian Head Band-Use long strip of black construction paper for the headband and have toddler clue on craft feathers or colorful feathers you cut from construction paper
- Corn Painting-roll ear of corn in paint that is spread on paper plate; have toddler roll the corn over white paper; use several corn cobs and several colors paint for pretty, textured art work
- Indian Bracelets-cut toilet roll in half and down the middle to make "clamp bracelets;" have toddler use markers, craft jewels/sequins, or glitter to decorate

Story Time
On Mother's Lap by Ann Herbert Scott
The Girl Who Loves Wild Horses by Paul Goble
The Legend of the Indian Paintbrush by Tomie DePaolo
The Very First Americans by Reading Railroad

Music
- Popcorn-play peppy music and let toddler jump up and down like "popcorn"
- Pass the feather – like hot potato game; when music stops whoever is holding the feather must give out an Indian war cry

Game Time
- Play with feathers; try to blow them to keep them in the air
- Picking Lemons: buy a bag of lemons (use later for lemonade); put basket on the opposite side of room; have child pick one lemon and bring across room to basket; continue until basket has been filled; toddlers will love this repetition especially if they think they are "helping" you to fill the basket(Color-yellow)

Snack Idea
- Tortilla Tee Pee-use Q-tips to "paint" food coloring onto flour tortilla, roll in cone shape and stand up to look like a tee pee; secure with a toothpick (this is more of an art project that uses food rather than a snack idea)
- Indian Painting-use white bread as your canvas and clean paintbrushes with food coloring to paint with; toast these "painting" and the colors will really become vibrant and yummy!
- Corn Bread
- Lemonade-use lemons from Game Time above

Fieldtrip Ideas
- Watch Pocahontas movie and eat popcorn
- Have a Native American guest speaker come in
- Visit an Indian museum if you have one nearby

Special Holiday Week
Letter: Review
Color: Yellow
Number: Review
Shape: Rectangle
Scripture: Now therefore, our God, we thank thee, and praise thy glorious name.
1 Chronicles 29:13

Theme: **Thanksgiving**

Bible

- Scripture: Now therefore, our God, we thank thee, and praise thy glorious name. 1 Chronicles 29:13
- Tell the story of the Ten Lepers: Jesus entered a village and met ten men who were lepers (sores on their skin) who were standing far off. They shouted and asked Jesus to heal them. Jesus healed them. Only one man turned back and thanked Jesus. List the things we should be thankful for. Pray and thank God now.

Theme Learning

- The First Thanksgiving – Pilgrims: The Pilgrims wanted to worship God the way they felt led to. They decided to go to America so that they could do so. They sailed on a boat called the Mayflower. 102 passengers were on the boat.
- The First Thanksgiving – Indians: the Pilgrims met the Indians; they were afraid at first, but the Indians were friendly; the Indians taught them to plant corn, get sap from trees, avoid poisonous plants, and catch fish in the rivers
- The First Thanksgiving – Feast: the Pilgrims and Indians came together for a feast; they probably ate venison (deer), fowl (birds), fish, vegetables and berries, corn bread… The feast lasted for 3 days
- Thanksgiving Today – we eat turkey, dressing, cranberry sauce, pumpkin pie, etc.; we get together to eat with family and friends; let each child share what they will do for Thanksgiving

Letter Skills

- Review Letters
- Review all letter boxes A – I (each week, fill empty wet wipes containers with things that begin with the letter of the week…you will have 26 boxes at the end of the year)
- Sing the Alphabet Song to review all letters
- Erase the letter – write letters learned so far on the board (A-I); have student come up and erase the letter you say; repeat so that everyone has a turn
- Pick a Pocket game – purchase one of those hanging shoe organizers with lots of pockets; put a letter in each (cut out from paper or use ABC magnets); children take turns coming up and pulling letter from pocket – he should tell what letter it is and what sound it makes

- Trace magnetic alphabet letters
- Alphabet stamping – purchase a set of ABC stamps and stamp pad and let the children stamp the letters on white paper
- Play dough with alphabet cookie cutters
- Sing: What's the Sound song to review all letters
  What's the Sound – tune B-I-N-G-O
  What's the sound that starts these words
  _____ and _____ and _____
  / / is the sound, / / is the sound, / / is the sound
  That starts ____, _____, and _____.

Math

- Review Numbers
- Flashlight Writing – turn off the lights and use a flashlight to "write" a number on the wall or ceiling; children must try to guess what number you wrote
- Who Has # __? game – give each child an index card that has a number on it; call out a number and those children who have it should stand; repeat several times and then let the children switch numbers with their neighbor
- Fishing for Numbers – provide a stick with yarn tied on one end; hot glue a magnet to the other end of the yarn; cut out fish shapes and add large metal gem clip at mouth; let children take turns fishing for the number you call out…or have them pull out a fish and tell you what number it is
- What Comes After game – call out a number and have children try to tell what number comes next…before

Shape Practice

- Thanksgiving Thank You Cards-give child construction paper which is shaped like a rectangle; fold it in half and discuss that now you have 2 rectangles; have child decorate with crayons and markers and give this Thank You card to someone special such as a Sunday School teacher

Color:

- Play with yellow play dough.
- Finger paint with yellow/red paint; notice how when mixed they make orange.
- Leaf Rubbings-take a walk and collect Fall leaves; place leaves under white paper and have toddler rub yellow or orange crayon over the leaf; the impression of the leaf veins will be on the paper; works best if you peel paper from crayon and use crayon sideways over the leaf…press down hard
- Jump On Color game – place sheets of construction paper in the middle of the Carpet; all out a color and select a child and instruct him to jump on the color and sit back down; repeat until everyone has a turn

Art

- Turkey Placemat-Purchase a cloth placemat in a light color (such as tan or pale yellow); paint toddler's hand to look like a turkey by painting the thumb and palm brown (body and head) and the fingers various Fall colors like pointer finger-red, tall finger-yellow, ring finger-orange; and pinky finger-green; use fabric markers to add eye and orange beak and to write Happy Thanksgiving; These will be keepsakes!

- Baby Food Jar Thanksgiving Candle Votive-cut orange, brown and yellow tissue paper into small square; have toddler paint glue onto outside of clean baby food jar and then stick tissue squares on the glue; when finished brush all over with glue to smooth down corners of tissue paper squares; when dry add tea light candle and place on Thanksgiving table for decoration
- Paper Bag Turkey-decorate brown lunch sack with markers; stuff with newspapers and twist end closed and up to resemble turkey head; glue on feathers cut from construction paper
- Paper Plate Collage: have toddler help you find pictures of foods he loves in magazines; cut them out and have toddler glue them on the paper plate
- Pillow Case Indian Vests – have children each bring in a twin size white pillow case (be sure to send this in a note in advance); cut the pillow case as shown; let children use markers or fabric paint to decorate

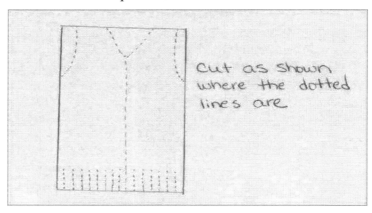

Music
- Turkey Pokey-like Hokey Pokey, but you put your drumsticks in, your tail feathers in, your beak in, wings in, etc.
- Dinner Bells-collect various bells and place in clean, plastic jar (like peanut butter jar); bells can be purchased in craft section of large retail store; secure the top and have child shake while you have music playing from the radio or a CD
- Falling Leaves-cut Fall leaves from construction paper; sing:
  - Leaves are falling down, won't you try and catch some.
    Leaves are falling down, won't you try and catch some.
    Leaves are falling down, won't you try and catch some.
    Catch some if you can! (throw leaves up and let them rain down)
- Thanksgiving Apple Pie Tambourines-use tin pie pans with apple seeds (or dry beans) inside; staple closed and secure edges with heavy tape to be sure no seeds escape; use as tambourines while you play lively music

Game Time

- Take a Fall walk- give toddler a brown paper sack or sand bucket and let him pick up "signs of Fall" such as colorful leaves, pine cones, and acorns (monitor carefully)
- Leaf Sorting-Place several shoeboxes on a table. Use different colored Fall leaves from Fall walk (above) and have your child sort the leaves according to color and place them into the right shoeboxes
- Build Pilgrim homes-play with blocks and "build" houses like the Pilgrims did
- Turkey Bean Bag Toss-draw large turkey with mouth open on poster board; tape the turkey to the back of a chair; have toddler try to toss beanbags into turkey mouth

Snack Idea

- Sugar Waffle Cone Cornucopia-add M&M's and mini marshmallows, Cheese Nips, etc. to the inside for a sweet and salty snack
- Pilgrim Hat-use vanilla wafer and mini marshmallow to make Pilgrim hats; secure marshmallow with a little frosting; you could always dip these in melted chocolate to look black like a real Pilgrim hat
- Cornucopias-Serve Bugles brand chips which look just like little cornucopias

Fieldtrip Ideas

- Invite parents for a Thanksgiving Meal; decorations made in Art and wear Indian vests made from pillow cases

J

Color: Green

Number: 4

Shape: Triangle

Scripture: …I am with you always, even unto the end of the world.   Matthew 28:20

Theme: **Jungle Safari**

Bible

- Scripture: …I am with you always, even unto the end of the world. Matthew 28:20
- Tell the story of Moses. Keep it simple: A mean Pharaoh (king) ordered all the Hebrew baby boys be killed. Moses' mother made a basket and put him in. She put the little basket boat into the river and asked her daughter, Miriam, to keep watch over the boat. Pharaoh's daughter found Moses and wanted to keep him. Miriam stepped out and said that she knew a lady who could care for Moses until he was bigger. Moses own mother got to take care of him. When Moses grew up, he was a great leader. He led God's people to the land God had promised them.
- Make boat from empty plastic container. Put small toy inside and float in bathtub

Theme Learning

- Discuss the Jungle-show Africa on a map or globe
- Discuss what a jungle looks like (have pictures available if possible)-lots of trees and plants, vines, etc.
- Jungle Safari Animals- lions, giraffes, hippopotamuses, rhinoceroses, elephants and zebras
- Discuss where the animals live in a safari-den, nests, burrow, hollow tree trunk, etc.

Letter Skills

- J says "j" like jump
- Play a Game: Write capital letter J and little j on separate index cards; also write various other letters already learned on cards; show cards one at a time and tell child to jump if he sees letter J.
- Decorate blank J with craft jewels or jewel stickers (*monitor for choking hazard)
- Letter J Hunt-look for and cut lots of letter J's from magazines and have toddler glue to paper (older toddlers can try to use safety scissors and cut the letters out themselves)
- Add Ants to the Anthill game – create an anthill using brown construction paper; tape this to the front of the circle area; cut out small black "ants" from construction paper; if child can say the correct sound that J makes when asked, he can come up and put an ant on the anthill; continue until everyone has had a turn; go back to those who didn't get it right the first time and let them try again so they can add an ant to the anthill

- J like a Jellyfish game – have each child, one at a time, say the "j" sound while bobbing up and down like a jellyfish

Math

- Number 4 Counting-write number 4 on piece of paper; have toddlers stick 4 stickers on the page; practice counting the stickers
- Homemade Dry Erase Board-place clear contact paper on top of white paper that has been glued to cardboard backing and you have an instant dry erase board; erases with baby wipe or damp rag; use *Vis A Vive* brand overhead projector markers for best results; 4's are easy to write since they are basically like writing number one three times; let toddlers practice on his very own dry erase board
- Make #4 using three popsicle sticks
- Repeat patterns for #4 – clap 4 times, blink 4 times, slap legs 4 times, pat back 4 times, etc.
- Number Flashcards – show number flashcards 1-10 and when children see #4 instruct them to jump up
- Four Corners – write the numbers 1 – 4 on while paper and post in the four corners of the room; write the numbers 1 – 4 on small pieces of paper and put them into a Ziploc bag; tell the children to go and stand in any corner; pull out a number from the bag and call it out; children in that corner must sit down; continue until only one (or a few) children is left.

Shape Practice

- Safari Triangle Hunt-tape triangles to wall using Painter's tape which comes off easily; give child flashlight and let him shine light on triangles around the room
- Triangle Stamping-cut triangle shape from sponge; let toddler stamp triangle shapes on paper
- Walk around the triangle – create a large triangle on the floor using blue painters tape or masking tape; have the children walk around the triangle

Color

- Colorful Clip Sorting-purchase colorful clothes pins ($1.00 type stores usually have colorful, easy open, plastic clothes pins); give child matching color paper glued to cereal box cardboard; let him put clothes pins of correct color on the cardboard; great fine motor activity

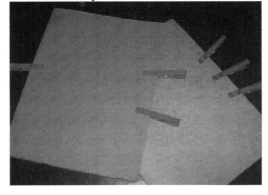

- Color Safari-provide several flashlights and instruct student to go on a color green hunt; shine light on things that are green around the room

Art
- Safari Binoculars-use toilet rolls taped together for jungle binoculars; decorate with markers or stickers…tape pictures of jungle animals all around the room and let children walk around with binoculars to spot them
- Yarn Lion Stick Puppet Mask-cut orange yarn into small strips; have toddler glue the strips to edge of paper plate; draw on nose and mouth and cut out eye holes; attach to Popsicle stick for a stick puppet or mask
- Scissor Skills Snake-have child decorate white paper plate with markers; draw lines in spiral fashion starting at edge and working your way in; help toddler use safety scissors to cut along the line; pick up center and the snake will hang down

Story Time
- <u>Starry Safari</u> by Linda Ashman
- <u>Bug Safari</u> by Bob Barner
- <u>ABC Safari</u> by Karen Lee
- <u>Go Diego, Go-The Great Jaguar Rescue</u> or any Diego books

Music
- Jungle Animal Movement-play lively music and have toddler move like snake, lion, frog, elephant, monkey, etc.
- Hot Monkey-play like Hot Potato and use any stuffed animal that you have at home; toss the animal back and forth with child; great gross motor activity

Game Time
- Jewelry Relay-have lots of costume jewelry out and have child put it on as fast as she can before timer dings; then just have fun dressing up; provide a safe mirror (boys may not want to put on jewelry and that's okay…you could explain that kings and queens used to wear lots of jewels)
- Jogging-use side walk chalk to write letter J outside; have toddler job around the letter J
- Jump on J-print J's on various pieces of colorful paper (cardstock is best or use solid placemats for more durability); have toddler jump from J to J
- Jungle Tent-use chairs and a sheet to create an instant jungle tent
- Jungle Trip-use large green poster board and draw a simple, curvy road using markers; if you are artistic decorate with simple jungle trees and grass sketching; give toddler a toy Hot Wheel type jeep and let him drive his jeep along the road on this instant jungle play mat
- Play Lion Says (like Simon Says)

Snack Ideas
- Animal Crackers
- Monkey Bananas-let children help cut bananas into ½ inch rounds using plastic disposable butter knife ; let toddler dip these into yogurt for an extra treat

Fieldtrip Ideas
- Watch movie, "The Jungle Book," or watch, "Go Diego, Go."

Special Holiday Week
Letter: Review
Color: Green
Number: Review
Shape: Triangle
Scripture: For unto you is born this day in the city of David a Saviour, which is
Christ the Lord. Luke 2:11

Theme: **Christmas Week**

Bible
- Scripture: For unto you is born this day in the city of David a Saviour, which is Christ the Lord. Luke 2:11
- Tell the Christmas story. Keep it simple: Mary and Joseph went to Bethlehem to be counted and pay taxes. When they got there it was crowded. They went from door to door (let toddler make knocking sound) and each time the inn or hotelkeeper said, "No room!" Finally one innkeeper let them stay in his stable or barn. Jesus was born that night

Theme Learning
- The First Christmas – Jesus Birth: A law was passed that said that everyone must return to the town where his family was from to be taxed. Mary and Joseph traveled to Bethlehem. Mary rode on a donkey. When they arrived, the town was busy. There were no rooms in the inn (like a hotel). An inn keeper told them they could stay in his stable (like a barn). Baby Jesus was born. Mary wrapped Him in cloth and laid Him in a manger (trough that animals would eat in).
- The First Christmas – Shepherds Visit: When Jesus was born, shepherds nearby had been watching their flock. An angel appeared to them. The angel told them not to be afraid. The angel told them that a baby had been born who was God's son….Christ the Lord. Suddenly many angels appeared and they sang praises to God. The shepherds left their sheep and hurried to go and see Jesus. They found Him in a manger in a stable. They worshipped Him.
- The Wise Men's Gifts: Some time later, Wise Men who had been following a star came to visit baby Jesus. They brought him gifts – gold (show example of ring), frankincense (something that when burned spells very good), and myrrh (like a perfume).
- Christmas Traditions today: Discuss what we do today to celebrate Christmas – Christmas tree, parade, Santa, stockings, presents, candle-light Christmas Eve services at church, Happy Birthday Jesus Christmas party, etc.

Letter Skills
- Review Letters covered so far
- Review all letter boxes A – J (each week, fill empty wet wipes containers with things that begin with the letter of the week…you will have 26 boxes at the end of the year)
- Sing the Alphabet Song to review all letters

- Erase the letter – write letters learned so far on the board (A-J); have student come up and erase the letter you say; repeat so that everyone has a turn
- Pick a Pocket game – purchase one of those hanging shoe organizers with lots of pockets; put a letter in each (cut out from paper or use ABC magnets); children take turns coming up and pulling letter from pocket – he should tell what letter it is and what sound it makes
- Trace magnetic alphabet letters
- Alphabet stamping – purchase a set of ABC stamps and stamp pad and let the children stamp the letters on white paper
- Play dough with alphabet cookie cutters
- Sing: What's the Sound song to review all letters
  What's the Sound – tune B-I-N-G-O
  What's the sound that starts these words
  _____ and _____ and _____
  / / is the sound, / / is the sound, / / is the sound
  That starts _____, _____, and _____.

Math
- Review Numbers covered so far
- Flashlight Writing – turn off the lights and use a flashlight to "write" a number on the wall or ceiling; children must try to guess what number you wrote
- Who Has # __? game – give each child an index card that has a number on it; call out a number and those children who have it should stand; repeat several times and then let the children switch numbers with their neighbor
- Fishing for Numbers – provide a stick with yarn tied on one end; hot glue a magnet to the other end of the yarn; cut out fish shapes and add large metal gem clip at mouth; let children take turns fishing for the number you call out…or have them pull out a fish and tell you what number it is
- What Comes After game – call out a number and have children try to tell what number comes next…before

Shape Practice
- Triangle Christmas Trees-cut triangles out of green construction paper; have toddler use Q-tip to dot on glue and add sequins, craft jewels, glitter, stickers, etc; attach magnet to back and hang on refrigerator
- Cookie Cutter Shape Match – trace cookie cutter shape onto old box and cut out with craft knife; have child put cookie cutters into correct shaped holes

Color
- Play with green play dough.
- Finger paint with green paint.
- Green Paper Plate Wreath-cut middle circle from paper plate; have toddler tear green paper into pieces and glue to plate; this will look like holly; add red circle cutouts for holly berries and hang

- Homemade wrapping paper or gift bag – decorate paper grocery sack and cut to use to wrap presents or leave in tact and use as a gift bag

Art
- Pine Cone Tree-save old milk jug cap and place play dough inside; stand pine comb upright and place stem part in play dough to resemble tree stand and to help the pine cone stay upright; have toddler use paintbrush to brush glue (be generous) on the pine cone; sprinkle with glitter; hot glue fun foam star or angel shape to the top
- Handprint Santa Ornament-use paintbrush to paint palm of toddler hand light pink; paint fingers white; paint thumb and top of hand red; press down to look like Santa's face

Music
- Sing Favorite Christmas Carols
- Jingle Bells-purchase jingle bells from craft department at large retail store; thread them onto pipe cleaner and twist end very securely; let your toddler shake the bells as you sing the song

Game Time
- Christmas Balloons-blow up green and red balloons and tie; have toddler try to toss and keep balloons in the air *monitor closely if balloon pops, the pieces pose a choking hazard
- Place several shoeboxes on the floor. Provide child with different, non-breakable Christmas ornaments. Have your child sort the ornaments according to size, color, or matching set.

Snack Idea
- Christmas Cookies – decorate with choice of colored icing (red, green, white…died with food coloring) and Christmas sprinkles
- Buy small box of animal crackers and wrap up in wrapping paper; let your child open his snack "present" today

Fieldtrip Ideas
- Visit a local Nursing Home and sing Christmas Carols; use the jingle bells made for Music; take The First Christmas Reindeer bookmarks/candy canes (see below) to pass out to the residents
- Have a Happy Birthday Jesus party

Christmas Gift Ideas
- Christmas Crayons-have toddler help break old crayons into pieces; be sure to peel paper from crayons before breaking; have toddler place pieces in Christmas themed muffin tins (or just regular mini muffin tin) that have been sprayed with nonstick cooking spray; melt in 200 degree oven for about 10 minutes or until melted; cool and pop out of tins; place in cellophane bag and add Christmas tag that reads, "Have a colorful Christmas!"
- Christmas Reindeer Bookmark and Candy Cane Gift
  - Print out the poem page on the next page on card stock (see Resource section for copy with multiple poems on one page)
  - Make a candy cane reindeer by using candy cane for body of reindeer and letting toddler twist brown pipe cleaner around crooked end to form antlers; have him use Q-tip to put dots of glue for eyes and nose; use wiggle eyes and take a hole puncher and punch out nose from fun foam or use small red pom pom; attach to bookmarks and give as gifts

The First Christmas Reindeer
I am a Christmas Reindeer.
I was grazing on a hill
When an angel appeared overhead.
It seemed the world stood still.

Shepherds who had seen the sight
Passed by me as they sang,
We're going to see the Son of God,
Who will forever reign.

At long last, we had arrived.
Our journey led us to a trough.
There we beheld a wondrous sight,
Baby Jesus-wrapped in swaddling cloth.

I was so moved by what I saw.
I wanted all to know.
So I began to run and run,
But, my legs just seemed too slow.

Then suddenly my legs felt light.
I was floating through the air.
It seemed I was now flying.
All below just looked and stared.

I sang out as I flew around,
God's only Son's been born.
He came to save the world from sin,
To rescue sin-sick and forlorn.

This is the story of how I became
A deer with wings it seems.
I still fly around all over
And of His praise I sing.

Merry Christmas!

K
Color: Blue
Number: 5
Shape: Star
Scripture: For where your treasure is, there will your heart be also. Luke 12:34

Theme: **Kings, Queens and Castles**

Bible

- Scripture: For where your treasure is, there will your heart be also. Luke 12:34
- Tell story of the Armor of God. Keep It Simple:
  - Belt of Truth-knowing what Jesus says is true and not believing any lies the devil may try to get you to believe
  - Breastplate of Righteousness-protect your heart by confessing sin
  - Sandals of Peace-be a peacemaker
  - Shield of Faith-shields against bad thoughts or temptations
  - Helmet of Salvation-Knowing you are saved protects your mind from doubts
  - Sword of the Spirit-Bible verses

Theme Learning

- What did kings and queens do? A king was the leader...kind of like the President. He had the responsibility of running his kingdom. If there was war, he would usually go and lead his army. If the king died, the queen would rule the kingdom. The queen would also run things when the king was away. The queen would also help with the children.
- What did kings and queens wear? robes, jewelry, fur, silk, crowns
- What did kings and queens eat? meat like beef and mutton (sheep), stews, breads, eggs, vegetables like peas and beans, fruits like apples, pears and plums.
- Where did kings and queens live? in a castle; a castle was fortified (protected) usually by a large wall, a moat (ditch filled with water all around the castle), and towers with arrowslits (tiny holes for soldiers to shoot arrows from)

Letter Skills

- Say It: K says "k" like a kangaroo
- Practice It: If child can say "k" sound when asked, he may stand and hop like a kangaroo
- Recognize It: Decorate Blank Letter K by gluing on kernels of rice inside outline or with "kisses" (lip stickers or stamp/stamp pad)
- Letter K box – fill empty wet wipes box with little things that start with K for kids to explore (small toy kitten, ketchup packet, key, etc.)
- Kleenex – Write K on a piece of construction paper; have children each tear a Kleenex into pieces and glue to the K outline

- Kiss if for kiss game – if child can say "k" sounds when asked, give him a Hershey's Kiss to eat
- K for kiss – Cut Hershey's Kiss shape from tin foil; have child glue to construction paper with paper tag strip that has letter K on it
- Letter K kangaroo pocket collection – create a "kangaroo pocket" by simple folding a piece of construction paper in half and stapling the sides; find and cut pictures of things that start with K from magazines and place in the pocket

Math
- King's Chest Counting-spray paint poker chips with gold spray paint; use for counting practice
- Stringing Necklaces-Kings and Queens love jewelry; string noodles, fruit loops, or cut straws on yarn to make necklaces; secure end of yarn with tape so it doesn't ravel
- Measure a Giant-find coloring page or draw picture of a "giant;" use Unifix cubes or other household item such as milk jug caps to measure how many caps tall the giant is (try to make giant 5 milk jug caps tall so that child can practice counting to 5)
- Counting Fingers – place colorful plastic toy rings on all 5 of your fingers and have the children count with you; let them count their own fingers as well; explain that we have 5 fingers on each hand and 5 toes on each foot
- Give me five – let children take turns giving their neighbors a high 5; let them each give you a high 5; have them count their fingers with you
- 5 Happy Kings finger play: hold up fingers as you say the following rhyme

   5 happy kings jumping on the bed
   One fell off and bumped his head
   The queen called the doctor and the doctor said, "No more kings jumping on the bed!"

   Repeat with 4 , 3, etc.

Shape Practice:
- Starry Night Search-hang paper stars around the room using painters tape which will come off easily; turn off lights and give toddler a flashlight; have him shine light around and try to find a star shapes around the room; let everyone have a turn to shine the light
- Shining Stars-let toddler put shiny star stickers onto black construction paper
- Make Star Wand-cut star shape from fun foam and taping to a straw; student could glue sequins or add glitter
- Star Stickers – place a star sticker on each child's hand; have him look at it and help count how many points (5)
- Sing *Twinkle, Twinkle, Little Star*; use Star Wand (above)

Color:
- Blues Clues coloring sheet-Google for Blues Clues coloring page and give child blue crayon and let him color Blue
- Play with Blue Play dough; kneed in sparkly glitter or foil confetti for a royal effect

Art:
- Kings/Queen Crown-ask Burger King to donate crown; turn it inside out so that blank side is facing up; let child glue on craft jewels, glitter, or decorate with markers
- Knight Helmets-make using clean milk jug; cover with aluminum foil
- Princess Hat-roll up colorful paper like cone; add streamers to top at point
- Knight's sword-cut sword shape from heavy cardboard; have child cover with aluminum foil to make shiny sword; make shield in the same way
- Sparkle Bottles-fill empty water bottle 2/3 with water; continue to fill the rest with vegetable oil; sprinkle in glitter, foil confetti, etc.; secure top with duct tape

Music:
- Key Jingling-give children sets of keys secured on key ring and let them jingle away as you play lively music; Home Depot will donate keys that were messed up when they were making keys
- Sparkly Jinglers-use sparkly pipe cleaners to string craft jingle bells to make a bracelet; play lively music and let child jingle away
- Jump inside the moat – put hoola hoops on the ground; play music; when it stops, children should jump inside the moats

Game Time:
- Make Sand Castles outside
- King and Queen Dress Up-buy crowns in party supply section; provide bathrobes and other props for dress up fun; drape purple cloth over chair for thrown
- Hunt for Gold-use gold coins from Numbers activity above; hide coins in sand box and tell child a dragon has hidden the coins they need to find them
- King/Queen May I (like Mother May I)
- King, King, Who has your Gold? game (like Doggy, Doggy, Where's Your Bone)– Have one child sit in chair with face away from the group; place a gold coin under chair; point to one child who quietly gets coin and hides in lap; King has three guesses to figure out who took the gold coin

Snack Idea:
- Tea Sandwiches-make sandwiches and cut with Toddler Bites Sandwich Cutter or cut sandwiches into small squares; serve juice in tea cups for a King and Queen tea party

- Royal Punch
  1 can Hawaiian Punch
  1/2 gallon pineapple sherbet
  2 - 2 liter bottles of ginger ale
  Freeze a can of Hawaiian Punch fruit juice until slushy. Pour into a punch bowl.
  Add ½ gallon pineapple sherbet and two bottles of ginger ale

Fieldtrip Ideas
- Watch movie, "The Lion King" or "Beauty and the Beast"
- Have someone dressed like a Disney Princess come and visit

L
Color: Blue
Number: 5
Shape: Star
Scripture: The entrance of thy words giveth light; it giveth understanding unto the
simple. Psalm 119:130

Theme: **Library and Books**

Bible:

- Scripture: The entrance of thy words giveth light; it giveth understanding unto the simple. Psalm 119:130
- Tell the story Jesus Heals a Blind Man. Keep it simple. A blind man was brought to Jesus. Jesus spat on his hands and touched the man's eyes. The man could see. Jesus healed the blind man.
- Blind fold child and play a version of pin the tail on the donkey

Theme Learning:

- Read Corduroy Goes to the Library; Discuss what a librarian does
- Talk about the library and what you will find there (computers, books, magazines, books on tape, movies, librarian)
- Discuss the kinds of books found at a library – fiction and nonfiction (fiction means not true and nonfiction means true)
- Discuss library cards and what you do to get one. Have an actual library application available to show the children. Discuss what's on the application…name, address, phone number, rules for checking out books)

Letter Skills:

- Say It: L says "l" like leaves
- Practice It: Cut leaf shapes from green construction paper; if children correctly say "l" sound when asked, throw leaves in air and let them rain down; have them help pick up and repeat
- Recognize It: Decorate Blank Letter L by gluing on leaves or ladybug stickers
- Lolipop activity – give each child a lollipop and practice making the "l" sound, ask, "What does L say?" Children respond and get to lick the lollipop once…repeat several time.
- Letter L book – staple several sheets of paper together. Write letter L with glue and have students sprinkle glitter on the glue for the front cover; make a leaf rubbing inside and write leaf; draw simple dots for eyes with two circles for glasses and write look; draw a heart and write love

Math:

- Lucky Charm Sorting-pour Lucky Charms cereal in bowl and have child pick out and sort the different marshmallows; all yellow stars together, all green clovers together, etc. (explain that Lucky is a fictional character)

- Goldfish Counting-divide paper into five sections; write numbers 1-5 on each section; provide gold fish crackers and let child put 1 in section labeled 1, 2 in section labeled 2, etc.
- Lady Bug Counting-cut out 5 red circles from construction paper; use black marker to draw dot 1-5 (1 dot on one, 2 dots on next one, etc.); cut out green leaf shapes and write numbers 1-5; child should match lady bug with number leaf by counting the lady bug's dots
- Leaf Toss – toss leaves in the air and instruct children to each count and pick up only 5; repeat several times
- Count the books – provide 5 children's picture books; show one at a time and count up to 5; repeat several times; count backwards from 5 to 1
- Repeat the Pattern (numbers 1-5) – have students repeat what you do; stop and count after each pattern: clap 5 times, slap legs 3 times, blink eyes 1 time, stomp feet 2 times, nod your head 4 times
- Repeat the Patter (number 5 only) – make 5 claps in different combinations and have the children repeat exactly as you clapped; for example,
  clap-clap……clap-clap-clap
  clap……..clap-clap-clap-clap

Shape Practice:
- Lucky Charm Stars-use stars from sorting activity above; glue to paper
- Use play dough and star cookie cutter to practice shape
- Star Frame-let child glue Popsicle sticks together to form star; glue child's picture in middle and put magnet on back
- Seeing Stars – place stars all over the room and various places and have children take turns using a paper towel roll "telescope" to spot a star

Color
- Paint the above Popsicle stick frames blue before or after gluing (once dry)
- Tint Foam Shaving Crème with washable blue paint and let child play in "blue snow"
- Purchase inexpensive blue gel toothpaste from dollar type store and squeeze into zip lock bag and seal tightly; spread around until flat inside bag and let child use finger to draw in the blue gel
- Blue Match – put a blue sticker on each child's hand (or just give each child a small blue construction paper square); have the children look around the room and find something that matches that color and bring it to the carpet to discuss; be sure to give time to go and put the item back
- Am I Blue? game – tell students that sometimes people say, "I am blue." to mean that they are sad today. Hold up pieces of colorful construction paper one at a time and instruct the children that when they see the color blue, they should make a sad face
- Blue's Clues – in advance place blue dog prints in a trail; have children follow the trail to find a blue treat to eat during Circle Time (blue M&M's, Blue's Clue's gummy treats, blue lollipop, etc.)

Art
- Make a Book-staple child's art work together to make a book; proudly add it to the bookshelf at home
- Make a Bookmark-cut two rectangles from clear contact paper; peel paper off one rectangle so that sticky side is up; let child sprinkle glitter or put confetti or sequins and top with other piece of contact paper; makes a beautiful bookmark

Music
- Quiet Music and Books-play quiet music and place a quilt on floor with lots of books for child to look at
- Read Bremen Town Musicians and act out story (Google for printable version)

Game Time
- Book Relay-place stack of books at one end and an empty laundry basket at other end; children must take turns picking up one book at a time, run to basket and drop it in; continue until all the books have been collected
- Favorite Books – in advance send a memo to parents telling them that the children can each bring in their favorite book; read these aloud to the class

Snack Idea
- Letter L biscuits-let child roll refrigerator biscuits into long snake like shape and then bend to form letter L; bake and enjoy
- Homemade Lemon Aid
- Graham Cracker Book-break graham cracker in half, but still place close together; spread with white icing; use tube icing to write "words" in book; place icing down center to show spine of book where the two cookies meet

Fieldtrip Ideas
- Take a trip to your county's library – call ahead and have the Children's Librarian read several books to the children and give them a tour of the library

M

Color: Blue

Number: 5

Shape: Star

Scripture: Pray without ceasing. 1 Thessalonians 5:17

Theme: **Mittens**

Bible

- Scripture: Pray without ceasing. 1 Thessalonians 5:17
- Tell the story of Mary and Martha. Keep it simple. Jesus came to visit his friends. Martha cooked and cleaned. Mary washed Jesus' feet with expensive perfume. She dried his feet with her long hair. Martha complained about doing all the work. Jesus told her that Mary was making the right choice by spending time with Him. We should not be so busy that we forget to spend time with God.
- Prayer Reminders: trace and cut out your child's hand print; tape all around the house to serve as reminders to stop and pray

Theme Learning

- Read – The Mitten by Jan Brett
- Discuss the animals in the book, The Mitten.; graph your favorite
- Discuss animals in winter: hibernation versus preparing for winter (some bears hibernate or go into a deep sleep during winter; some store up food; some grow extra fur to stay warm…)
- Mittens Matter Hot/Cold Experiment-put one mitten on each child's hand; leave the other bare; place a piece of ice in each hand; discuss hot/cold (if you don't have enough mittens so that each child can have one, just have several and take turns..or ask parents in advance to bring child's mittens to school)

Letter Skills

- M says "m" like mitten
- Play a Game: string up a piece of yarn between two chairs or on the wall; provide colorful clothes pins; cut out mitten shapes from construction paper; take turns have the children say the "m" sound when asked; if correct, he may put a mitten on the clothes line using a clothes pin (be sure to go back to those who don't say it correctly and give them a chance to say it correctly and put up a mitten)
- Decorate blank M with markers. Try making rainbow stripes.
- Mitten Lacing-cut mitten shape from construction paper and mount on cereal box cardboard; punch holes around mitten and use shoelace to "sew" around edges; write letter M on the mitten using glitter puff paint or glitter glue
- M is for Mountain – cut out an M from construction paper, have children glue the M to another piece of construction paper add glue cotton balls (torn and stretched) at the top of the points to look like snow at the tops of two mountains; write mountain at the bottom; have child underline or circle the m in mountain

Math
- Draw With Ice: use ice cube on sidewalk to practice writing number 5
- Ice Fishing for Numbers-cut out fish shapes and write numbers 1-5; slip gem clip on end of fish; attach string to end of wooden spoon; add magnet to end of string; call out a number and let child try to fish for it
- Counting Snowballs-provide 5 white Styrofoam craft balls and count together; give 5 children a snowball to hold and have them bring it up when asked as you count together; count backwards by handing the snowballs out again to different children; repeat until everyone has had a turn
- 5 Little Mittens song/fingerplay – say poem and hold up fingers
  5 Little Mittens (tune of: 5 Little Indians)
  1 little, 2 little, 3 little mittens
  4 little, 5 little, really warm mittens
  Red mittens, blue mittens, and some green mittens
  Help keep our hands warm
- Mitten Pretend – have children put on pretend mittens; have them put hands up in the air and shake their mittens 5 times; pat their legs 5 times; clap 5 times; etc.
- Yarn Mitten – draw a mitten shape onto white paper and make copies for each child; cut 5 small pieces of yarn for each child and have him glue inside the mitten shape; count the pieces of yarn and write number 5 on the paper

Shape Practice
- Shiny Star Play Dough Shapes-Need shiny glitter into white play dough; use star shaped cookie cutter
- Count the Points on a Star-for shape and math practice, count the points on a 5 point construction paper star; glue on 5 shiny squares of tin foil to each point (cut in advance)
- Compare mitten with star – how are they alike/different; the star has 5 points and the mitten has 5 fingers…are they the same or different color?...

Color
- Colored Ice - color water with blue food coloring and fill ice trays; once frozen place in large zip lock bag; toddler can play with the frozen blue cubes without getting wet; be sure to use this opportunity to point out that the ice is melting and turning back to blue water; also point out how difference between hot/cold
- Mitten Match-hang yarn clothesline between two chairs; but out a use clothes pins to attach mittens in various colors; have child try to put matching mitten beside each other
- Find the Blue Mitten – hold up mittens one at time that have been cut from construction paper in advance; when child sees the blue mitten, s/he should clap hands
- Mitten Hide and Seek – hide blue mittens cut from construction paper all around the room and let children take turns going to find one an bringing it back to the circle

Art
- Styrofoam Ball Snowman-purchase 3 Styrofoam craft balls for each child; have child poke toothpick halfway into one ball and then have him put another ball on top of toothpick that is sticking up; repeat to form snowman; add fun foam eyes, carrot nose, mouth and buttons; add toothpick arms and a piece of felt for a scarf
- Mitten decorating-cut out large mitten shape from blue construction paper; have precut fabric squares available for child to glue onto mitten to decorate; glue cotton balls for the part where wrist would be for a cute finish

Music
- Sing, "Twinkle, Twinkle Little Star"-(shape practice); make fun foam star shapes and tape to straws or unsharpened pencils for children to move during the song
- Dress Up Relay – play fast tempo music and place winter clothes in front of child; when music starts, have him quickly dress himself with hat, coat, mittens, boots, scarf…play music again and let child quickly take winter clothes off (Note: you can just use mittens..children must put on and take off)

Game Time
- Snow Ball Fight-ball up white paper and have a "snow ball fight" (instruct them to only aim low); have children help clean up
- Shaving Crème Snow-squirt white shaving crème on the kitchen table and let your child have fun playing in the "snow"
- Pretend Ice Skating-put two paper plates under feet and skate (or really scoot) away
- Mitten Toss – create bean bags using mittens (or simply stuff with fiberfill pillow stuffing); let children try to ring a laundry basket with the bean bag mittens
- Kittens Lost Mittens game – have three children come to the front of the circle and sit in chairs facing away from the other children; place a mitten under each chair; point to the 3 students who will come up and quietly take mitten and hide in lap; say, "Kittens, Kittens, who took your mittens?"; children in chairs each must turn around and try to guess who took their mitten; repeat until everyone has had a turn

Snack Idea
- Marshmallow snowman-use white frosting to stick 3 marshmallows together; also use frosting to add mini chocolate chips for eyes and buttons; add pretzels for arms

Fieldtrip Ideas
- Have someone who can knit come in and give a demonstration and talk to the kids about how mittens are made
- Visit a farm and see sheep; talk about how the yarn for mittens comes from sheep wool

N
Color: Blue
Number: 5
Shape: Star
Scripture: Oh taste and see that the Lord is good: blessed is the man that trusteth in Him.
Psalm 34:8

Theme: **Nutrition & Health**

Bible:
- Scripture: Oh taste and see that the Lord is good: blessed is the man that trusteth in Him. Psalm 34:8
- Tell the story of The Prodigal Son. Keep it simple. Jesus told the story of a father who had two sons. One day his younger son said he wanted his share of the family money fortune. As soon as he had the money, he left home. While the older son stayed home, the younger traveled and spent his money on fancy clothes and jewels and parties. When he had no money left, he could no longer buy good food. He got a job feeding pigs. He was so hungry that he realized that even the pigs were eating better than he. He was sorry. He returned home. His father forgave him and gave him a special ring to show him he was welcome back. Jesus told this story so that we will know that he loves us no matter what we do.
- Feed the Pig-draw pig on manila file folder; cut hole for mouth, stand it upright; let child put yellow squares cut from construction paper (corn) into pigs mouth

Theme Learning
- 5 Food Groups – print a copy of the food group plate from the following website: www.choosemyplate.gov (the pyramid has now been replaced with a plate design)

- Discuss fruits/vegetables – show pictures of examples…sort fruits from vegetables
  Any fruit or 100% fruit juice counts as part of the Fruit Group. Fruits may be fresh, canned, frozen, or dried, and may be whole, cut-up, or pureed.

  Any vegetable or 100% vegetable juice counts as a member of the Vegetable Group. Vegetables may be raw or cooked; fresh, frozen, canned, or dried/dehydrated; and may be whole, cut-up, or mashed.
  Copied from www.choosemyplate.gov

- Discuss grains – show pictures of examples
  Any food made from wheat, rice, oats, cornmeal, barley or another cereal grain is a grain product. Bread, pasta, oatmeal, breakfast cereals, tortillas, and grits are examples of grain products. Copied from www.choosemyplate.gov

- Discuss proteins & dairy – show pictures of examples
  All foods made from meat, poultry, seafood, beans and peas, eggs, processed soy products, nuts, and seeds are considered part of the Protein Foods Group. Beans

and peas are also part of the Vegetable Group.

All fluid milk products and many foods made from milk are considered part of this food group.
Copied from www.choosemyplate.gov

Letter Skills:
- Say It: N says "n" like nest
- Play a Game: Spread a sheet on the floor and scrunch up the ends to make it circular and with a raised edge like a bird's nest. Have toddler pretend to be baby bird. When he says "n" sound he may get into the nest; have him "fly away" and then make him say "n" sound to get back to seat
- Decorate Blank Letter N by spreading a thick layer of glue all over letter and having toddler sprinkle crunched up Wheat Cereal or straw to look like a nest
- N is for Numbers collage – find numbers in magazines, cut and glue to construction paper for a numbers collage; write numbers at the bottom and have child circle the letter n
- Pin the Nose on the Baker – draw a simple face on paper; add a white chef hat cutout at the top; provide colorful circles for the nose; if child can say "n" sound when asked, s/he can come up and be blindfolded and try to Pin the Nose on the Baker (Note: use a child-sized night mask for the blindfold…saves time so you don't have to tie a blindfold every time)
- N is for Nest with Baby Bird – provide a large man's sized white t-shirt; if child can say "n" sound when asked, s/he can sit on floor and crunch down inside white t-shirt (like egg) and then when we count 1,2,3, s/he cracks out of the egg
- N is for Necktie craft – explain to children that sometimes when you go to nice restaurants, you dress up; cut a necktie shape from construction paper and let children decorate with markers (stripes) or polka dots or fabric scraps, etc.

Math:
- Counting Apples-apples are great nutritional snacks and are also great counters; purchase a small back and practice counting them
- Pretzel Counting-use stick pretzels for counting; use the pretzels to make the numbers 1-5 (for Circle time-give each child 5 pretzels, let them count and eat)
- Meal Sorting-Cut various foods from magazines; have child sort them according to breakfast, lunch, and dinner
- Baking & Counting – have children pretend to hold bowl and stir with spoon; stir 5 times to the right; stir 5 times the opposite way; taste the batter 5 times (smack lips 5 times); fill 5 muffin tins; turn stove on (5 clicks); hear 5 beeps from kitchen timer (beep-beep-beep-beep-beep)
- Give Me Five – let children give neighbor 5; practice right and left…give neighbor on your left a high five…give neighbor on your right a high five; repeat "up high" and "down low"

Shape Practice:

- Play Dough Baking-use play dough, rolling pin, cookie cutters to "bake" nutritional foods (don't forget to use star cookie cutter for shape practice)
- 5 Star Restaurants – tell children that restaurants are graded on how good they are; a really good restaurant will receive 5 stars; a poor restaurant will receive 1 star; call out the name of a restaurant and let children hold up fingers for the number of stars they would rate the restaurant
- Pretzel Star – show children how you can make a star using pretzels

Color:

- Muffin Tin Sorting-tape colorful circles in bottom of muffin tin; have toddler put matching crayon into correct muffin cup
- Color Sorting-provide various colors of construction paper; place food pictures of that same color on top (or use toy food items); example: banana and corn on yellow
- Make simple muffin flashcards by drawing muffin shape on index card; add different colored dots to each one; instruct children that when they see the blue berry muffin they should yell, "Blueberry!"

Art:

- Food Pyramid-Draw large triangle on paper; have child help find good foods in magazine and cut out pictures to place on food pyramid; Google food pyramid to see what goes where (you may choose to use the updated plate design that has now replaced the pyramid...use a paper plate divided with a marker...put the dairy on the back of the plate)
- Food Stamping-use apples, potatoes, broccoli tops, etc. dipped in paint to stamp onto white paper
- Paper Plate Healthy Lunch collage-glue magazine pictures onto paper plate to show a healthy, balanced lunch

Music:

- Sing, "Old McDonald Had a Farm"- change the song slightly and sing "and in his garden he had a carrot, and say yum, yum, yum, yum, yum instead of e-i-e-i-o"
- Bean Maraca-add dry beans to empty juice concentrate can or Pringles cans and reseal; secure with tape; play lively music and let the children play their maraca's

Game Time:

- Set the Table-using large construction paper or two smaller pieces taped together, trace a plate, napkin, fork, spoon, knife, and cup in the correct spaces; have child decorate; use as placemats at lunch (Note: fork on left; knife then spoon on right of plate)
- Play Restaurant-save old paper take out menus and let child be the waiter as you order food
- Exercise is Healthy - jumping, running, kicking, throwing, touching toes, etc.

Snack Idea:

- Make a pizza-often pizza restaurants will set up a fieldtrip for groups of children during their daytime hours when they aren't as busy; we've been before and they let everybody make their own personal pizza; or just purchase pre-made pizza crusts and all the fixings.
- Bread Taste Test-Use Toddler Bites Sandwich Cutter to cut several flavors and varieties of breads into small pieces; have a taste test
- Healthy Trail Mix – let children mix mini marshmallows, M&M's, popcorn, and pretzels together and put in Ziploc baggie

Fieldtrip Ideas

- Farmers Market
- Have a dietician come and speak (your local hospital will have one that will probably be willing to come in and talk with the class…you could also ask your school system's nutritionist)
- Make Pizza – Dominos pizza and many other chain pizza stores will allow children to for a fieldtrip; they will each make their own individual pizza
- Grocery Store – look for nutritious foods; have the produce worker talk about fruits and vegetables

O
Color: Pink
Number: 6
Shape: Heart
Scripture: Follow me, and I will make you fishers of men. Matthew 4:19

Theme: **Ocean**

Bible
- Scripture: Follow me, and I will make you fishers of men. Matthew 4:19
- Tell the story of, The Great Catch. Keep it simple: Peter and some other fishermen had been fishing all night long and had caught nothing. Jesus told them to cast their net again. They obeyed and their net was full of fish. Peter believed in Jesus and became one of his helpers. Peter became a fisher of men.
- Box Boat-provide old box so that child can pretend he is in the boat; put gem clips on fish cutouts and stick with yarn and magnet on end and let child "fish" from the "boat"

Theme Learning
- Discuss the Ocean – another name for the ocean is the sea; show map of USA or globe; explain that the Pacific Ocean is on the left side and the Atlantic Ocean is on the right side; there are five major oceans in the world: Atlantic, Pacific, Indian, Arctic, and Southern (Antarctic) Ocean (show these on the globe if you'd like)
- Ocean Salt Water – the ocean has salt water in it; fish in the ocean can live in this salty water; people cannot drink the water from the ocean because it would make them sick; let children taste a tiny amount (about 1 tablespoon) of salt water in small paper cups
- Types of Fish in the Ocean – show pictures of fish that live in the ocean (clown fish, dolphins, sharks, etc.)
- Other Creatures in the Ocean – show pictures of other creatures that live in the ocean (whales, sting ray, crabs, octopus, sponges, etc.)
- Long O sound – o can say "o" like ocean; what are some other words that start with long o sound (open, okay,

Letter Skills
- Say it: O says "o" like the sound you make at the doctor when you have a sore throat and he says, "Say open up and say ahhh."
- Play a Game: Children take turns saying "ahhh" sound when asked what O says
- Decorate blank O with cheeriOs; draw or print outline of letter O; glue on cheerios cereal
- O is for Octopus – cut letter o shape from construction paper; have child glue O to another piece of construction paper; add streams at the bottom for tenticles; add two wiggly eyes at the top; write octopus on the bottom and have child circle letter o

- Sand writing practice: pour small amount of sand in shallow baking pan; have toddler use finger to practice writing letter O

Number Skills
- Sand writing practice: pour small amount of sand in shallow baking pan; have toddler use finger to practice writing number 6
- Seashell Counters: use 6 sea shells for counting practice (can be purchased in craft section of large retail stores)
- Number Diving – write the numbers 1 through 6 on fish shapes; spread them in the middle of the carpet; call one child at a time to "swim" to the middle and pick up the number you call out; repeat several times
- Caught a Shark Alive poem/fingerplay
  1,2,3,4,5…I caught a <u>shark</u> alive
  6,7,8,9,10…I let him go again
  (Repeat with other creatures from the ocean)
- Number 6 Hermit Crab Shell – wite number 6 on construction paper; make it look like a hermit crab shell; glue a hermit crab

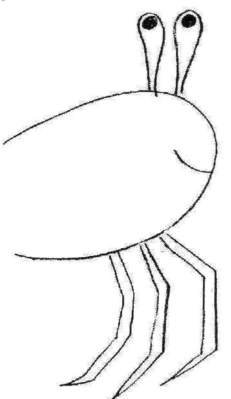

Hermit Crab Template

Finished Crab Picture

Shape Practice
- Heart Fish: Cut a large heart and two small hearts from construction paper; have your toddler help assemble the fish-large heart is body, one small heart for tail, and one small heart for fin; decorate with crayons
- Heart Exchange - pass out colorful heart shaped cutouts and have children exchange

Color
- Chalk Picture: use pink colored chalk to draw a picture on black construction paper
- Red and White make pink: make pink paint having toddlers stir red and white paint together; use pink paint to paint a white heart cutout to give grandparent, neighbor, etc.
- Demonstrate how red and white paint make pink – add white paint to water in a glass; add drops of red paint one a time; stir after each drop; count to see how many red drops it takes to make the water turn pink
- Make a list of pink things – list as many things that children can think of that are pink (flowers, bubblegum, ballet shoes, pigs, ham, dress, etc.)

Art
- Ocean in a bottle: fill a plastic water bottle with 2/3 water and tint with blue food coloring; add baby oil or vegetable oil ½ inch from top of bottle; add tiny shells, small fish cut from fun foam, glitter, etc; close top tightly; toddler can rock bottle back and forth and see waves.
- Fish with Scales: make a simple fish cutout from construction paper; cut circle stickers in half (price stickers found in office supply section of large retail stores); these half circles will represent scales; have toddler stick these on fish cutout
- Paper Plate Jellyfish: Decorate paper plate or simply use colored paper plate; have toddler glue precut strips of streamers to the plate; add large wiggly eyes

Music
- Rain Stick: Fill empty Pringles can with dry beans; taped top closed securely using duct tape; have toddler shake the rain stick slowly like a gently rain…fast like a storm, etc.

Game Time
- Beach Ball Bowling: set up 2 Liter Soda Bottles like bowling pins; have toddlers use beach ball like bowling ball to knock pins down (check local Recycling Center if you need empty soda bottles)
- Kiddie Pool Playground: purchase large, plastic kid's size pool (if out of season, check a local flea market or yard sale); add stuffed animals and other toys to this playground; you could also opt to purchase large playground balls (the ones that use to be in restaurant play areas) and add them to the tub
- Wash the windows: fill spray bottles with water and give each toddler a rag; have him "wash" the windows; praise his helpfulness
- Swim in the Ocean – provide a blue sheet for this game; let each child pick up part of the edge and lift sheet; explain that this is the ocean; gently lift up and down to make waves; call out two children's names; they must "swim" under the sheet (ocean) and switch places; continue until everyone has a turn

Snack Ideas
- Sand Pudding: place vanilla crème cookies (like Oreos) in large Ziploc bag and crush into fine pieces that will look like sand; make vanilla pudding and sprinkle with "sand"
- Ocean Shakes: Pour ½ cup cold milk into sealable container; add 1 tablespoon blue colored gelatin; add 8 oz. container of yogurt; use Toddler Bites Banana Slicer to slice banana into slices and add to shake; use blender or hand mixer to mix well; pour back into sealable container and let your toddler shake his own smooth some more; the blue gelatin will make the shake look blue like the ocean

Fieldtrip Ideas
- Visit aquarium (if you live nearby)
- Watch the movie, "Nemo."
- Visit pet store with fish

P

Color: Pink

Number: 6

Shape: Heart

Scripture: And God said, Let the earth bring forth grass, the herb yielding seed, and
the fruit tree yielding fruit… Genesis 1:11

Theme: **Plants**

Bible:
- Scripture: And God said, Let the earth bring forth grass, the herb yielding seed,
and the fruit tree yielding fruit… Genesis 1:11
- Tell the Creation Story. Keep it simple. Go over the Days of Creation using the
list below. Spend time discussing the grass, trees, and plants God made.
    - Day 1- Day & Night
    - Day 2- Sky
    - Day 3- Land & Sea
    - Day 4- Sun, Moon, & Stars
    - Day 5- Fish & Birds
    - Day 6- Animals and Man
    - Day 7- God rested

Theme Learning
- Discuss what plants need in order to grow: seed, soil, water, sunlight, carbon
dioxide
- Discuss seeds – show different kinds
- Discuss soil/dirt & water
Plants need water in order to grow; tiny tubes within the plants help carry water
throughout the plant; place a celery stalk in a jar of water; add several drops of
food coloring; observe each day to see the celery turn the color of the water
starting at the bottom and eventually even turning the leaves on top
- Discuss roots – roots are like straws; they suck the water up from the ground; let
one child come up and demonstrate by sucking up water from a glass using a
straw
Discuss carbon dioxide – the air that we breath out is called carbon dioxide; plants
need this to live

Letter Skills:
- Say It: P says —p̆ like a puff of air
- Play a Game: Let child make —p" sound to get a turn to blows bubbles
- Decorate Blank Letter P with polka dots-use circle stickers, Q-tips with paint, or
the eraser end of a pencil dipped in paint to make the dots
- Letter P Box – add small items that start with P to an empty wet-wipes boxes
labeled with the letter P (popcorn, penny, pencil, safety pen, toy pig, etc.)

- P like Popcorn – show flashcards of letters learned so far; when child sees letter P, s/he should jump up like a piece of popcorn popping; keep putting letter P back into the deck so that the children have lots of changes to pop
- Write letter P on construction paper; trace the letter with glue and add popcorn
- Letter P Collage – look through magazines and find things that start with P; glue to construction paper

Math:
- Seed Sorting-provide different types of seeds to sort
- Flower Pen Writing-make a special pen (or pencil) for your child to practice writing the number 6 with; use green florist tape to tape a single artificial flower to the end of the pen; finish wrapping the florist tape around the pen to the end
- Index Card Flashcards-Write numerals 1-6 each on one index card; have toddler glue on the number of seeds listed on the card
- Seed Packet Match-turn duplicate empty seed packs into matching game
- Flower Counting – use artificial flowers to practice counting; give 6 children a flower; count and let them add their flower to a vase; count backwards to remove; repeat until everyone has had a turn
- Roll the Dice – let children take turns rolling the dice until someone lands on 6; count the dots; repeat until everyone has at least one turn

Shape Practice:
- Heart Sequencing-provide several sizes hearts cut from construction paper; have child put them in order by size
- Sprinkle flour in shallow cookie sheet and have child practice drawing hearts with finger
- Heart Search – hide hearts all around the room and let children take turns going to find them and bringing them back to the circle; sort them by colors
- Draw Hearts with Finger – use your finger to draw a heart shape on the person on your right's back; turn to the person on your left and draw a heart on his back with your finger; repeat several times
- Heart Burn game – show shape flashcards; when children see the heart, they should groan and rub tummy as if they have heart burn

Color:
- Print Handprint Flower-trace child's hand on pink construction paper and cut out; have toddler glue on green stem and leaves (cut from construction paper)
- Muffin Liner Flowers-have toddler glue pink muffin liners to blue paper in the position in which it would sit in muffin pan; paint Popsicle stick green and glue on for stem and draw on leaves

Art:
- Paper Cup Face with Grass Hair-draw face on small, white Styrofoam cup; add soil and grass seeds close to top; the seeds will grow within a matter of days and

will create hair for your cup person; let toddler use safety scissors to give him a hair cut
- Grow a potato-fill a clean jelly jar with water; pierce potato in sides with toothpicks and place on top of the jar opening (the toothpicks help the potato from falling in the jar); observe the roots grow down into the jar over the next few weeks and the leaves growing up on top Note: bottom of potato must always be immersed in water
- Terra Cotta Decorating-let toddler use paint brushes and colorful paint to decorate small terra cotta pot (usually cost less than $1 in Gardening section); have him plant flower seeds and give to loved one for Valentine's Day
- Egg Carton garden-purchase 12 different packs of seeds that toddler helps pick out; let him plant one seed in each of the different egg carton cups; over the next weeks, he can observe how each different seed looks/grows differently

Music:
- Streamers-tape long streamer to end of wooden spoon; let child twist and turn it while music plays
- Sandpaper Blocks-glue 2 pieces sandpaper to 2 wooden blocks; rub together as music plays

Game Time:
- Water Play-discuss how plants need water to grow; provide a large bucket of water on a vinyl, water proof table cloth; provide lots of cups; bowls, measuring cups, spoons, etc. for water fun
- Act out growing from seed to plant – get really small in a ball—sit up—get up on knees—stand hunched over—stand up—stretch out arms

Snack Idea:
- Dirt Pie-fill small Styrofoam cup with chocolate pudding; have child help crush chocolate sandwich type by placing inside zip lock bag and double bagging; hit with toy wooden block; sprinkle crushed cookies which will look like soil over the pudding; let toddler add M&M —seds"; add gummy worm (for older children)
- Vegetable Stew-open cans of the following and let toddler pour cans into a crock pot: 1 can Corn, 1 can Green Beans, 1 can Diced Potatoes, 1 can Diced Carrots, 1 can Diced, Seasoned Stewed Tomatoes (undrained), half small onion (minced), 1 lb. Ground Beef (browned and drained), Salt and Pepper to taste

Fieldtrip Ideas
- Visit a local nursery

Special Holiday Week
Letter: Review
Color: Red
Number: Review
Shape: Heart
Scripture: …Love one another; as I have loved you...
John 13:34

Theme: **Valentine's Week/Love**

Bible

- Scripture: …Love one another; as I have loved you… John 13:34
- Tell story of the Good Samaritan. Keep it simple: A man was walking along the road. Some men robbed him and he was hurt. Three people passed by, but only the third man stopped to help. He bandaged the man's hurt places and gave him money to stay in a hotel until he was better.
- Have child place band aids on doll or stuffed animal to roll play how the Good Samaritan took care of the man in the story.
- Discuss helping others. Have child help you clean up by using large laundry basket and having him pick up toys around house. Let your child pass out the napkins at supper.

Theme Learning

- Who was Saint Valentine? It is believed that Saint Valentine was a priest in Rome who helped Christians who were persecuted during that time (there are other legends about who this Saint was)
- Who Do You Love? Talk about what it means to love someone. Who do you love? How can you show love to others?
- Valentine's Day Traditions Today: candy, parties, flowers, hearts, balloons, card exchange, etc.
- Valentine Cards Through the Years: show examples (if possible, from different eras)

Letter Skills

- Review Letters covered so far
- Review all letter boxes A – P (each week, fill empty wet wipes containers with things that begin with the letter of the week…you will have 26 boxes at the end of the year)
- Sing the Alphabet Song to review all letters
- Erase the letter – write letters learned so far on the board (A-P); have student come up and erase the letter you say; repeat so that everyone has a turn
- Pick a Pocket game – purchase one of those hanging shoe organizers with lots of pockets; put a letter in each (cut out from paper or use ABC magnets); children take turns coming up and pulling letter from pocket – he should tell what letter it is and what sound it makes

- Trace magnetic alphabet letters
- Alphabet stamping – purchase a set of ABC stamps and stamp pad and let the children stamp the letters on white paper
- Play dough with alphabet cookie cutters
- Sing: What's the Sound song to review all letters
  What's the Sound – tune B-I-N-G-O
  What's the sound that starts these words
  _____ and _____ and _____
  / / is the sound, / / is the sound, / / is the sound
  That starts ____, _____, and _____.

Math
- Review Numbers covered so far
- Flashlight Writing – turn off the lights and use a flashlight to "write" a number on the wall or ceiling; children must try to guess what number you wrote
- Who Has # __? game – give each child an index card that has a number on it; call out a number and those children who have it should stand; repeat several times and then let the children switch numbers with their neighbor
- Fishing for Numbers – provide a stick with yarn tied on one end; hot glue a magnet to the other end of the yarn; cut out fish shapes and add large metal gem clip at mouth; let children take turns fishing for the number you call out…or have them pull out a fish and tell you what number it is
- What Comes After game – call out a number and have children try to tell what number comes next…before

Shape Practice
- Heart Hide and Seek: Hide heart cutouts all over the room and let your toddler go on a heart hunt.
- Purchase heart shaped stickers readily available around Valentine's Day. Give your child a piece of construction paper and let him put the stickers all over it.

Color
- Play with red play dough.
- Finger paint with red paint.
- Stained Glass Heart hanging: Purchase colorful tissue paper and clear contact paper. Have your toddler tear tissue paper into small pieces. Precut the tissue paper into small squares if you would rather. Have toddler place red tissue paper pieces on sticky side of one piece of contact paper. When finished, add piece of contact paper on top and smooth out with hand. Cut out in the shape of a heart. Punch a hole and attach a piece of red yarn. Hang in a window for a stained glass heart.

Art
- Make Valentine Cards: provide lots of supplies and stickers and let children get creative

- Valentine Card Bucket: Ask a local restaurant or school lunchroom to save large vegetable cans for you. Wash the cans out and spray paint red, white or pink. Drill two holes on either side of the can. Let your child add fun foam hearts, heart stickers, or decorate with paint and sponge shapes. Add ribbon through the drilled holes to make a handle. Have children bring in Valentines to exchange. Be sure each bucket is clearly labeled with child's name. Send home a class list for parents in advance.

Music
- Teach sign language for *I love you*: open hand wide; put tall finger and ring finger down
- Teach sign language for Jesus Loves Me and sing while signing: for Jesus you point to the palms of each hand…one and then the other using tall, middle finger; for loves you cross your arms in front of your chest; for me just point to yourself
- Sing: "Jesus Loves the Little Children." Use sign language for word love.

Game Time
- Place several shoeboxes on a table. Fill them with different colored construction paper hearts cut into a variety of sizes. Have your child sort the hearts according to size, color, or both.
- Blow Kisses: Toddlers LOVE blowing kisses. Blow a kiss to your toddler and have him blow one back. Repeat over and over. Try up high, down low, to the right, left, etc.
- Valentine Bingo – see Resource section for game board and pieces

- A Tisket, A Tasket game – provide a basket with heart cut out; have the children form a circle; give one child the basket and have him walk around the outside of the circle as we sing the following; he should drop the heart and see if that child can catch him before he gets back to his seat (run around outer circle much like you do for the game Duck, Duck, Goose)

A Tisket, A Tasket song

A tisket, a tasket, a green and yellow basket
I wrote a letter to my friend
And on the way I dropped it

- Who Stole My Heart? Game – played like Doggy, Doggy, Where's Your Bone; have children sit in circle; one child sits in chair facing away from others; place a heart cut out under chair; point to one child who quietly comes up and gets heart and hides between legs; everyone says, "Who Stole Your Heart?" and the child in chair turns around and has three guesses

Snack Idea

- Hershey's Kisses & pretzels make a sweet and salty treat
- Cupcakes with red sprinkles: Make cupcakes with white frosting. Buy red sugar sprinkles and let your toddler shake away. This is messy, but so much fun for your toddlers. He/she will be so proud of the cupcake he helped decorate. Older preschoolers may be able to frost their own cupcake with plastic butter knife.

Fieldtrip Ideas

- Visit a local Nursing Home and sing songs, pass out Valentine Cards
- Have a Valentine's Day Party

Valentine's Day Gift Ideas

- "Here's a little something sweet to make your breakfast toast a treat!" Have your child mix sugar and cinnamon together in large plastic mixing bowl. Let him spoon the mixture into clean baby food jars. Place fabric circle or seasonal cupcake liner on top of lid. Wrap with rubber band and then tie with pretty ribbon or yarn. Attach a card with message above. Give to grandparents, elderly neighbor, friends, etc. as Valentine's Day gift.
- "You're Cut Out to Be My Valentine" Have your child decorate a precut heart shape tag with message above written on it. Use ribbon to attach to heart shaped cookie cutter. Give as a gift to church teachers, grandparents, etc.
- "Dough you want to be my Valentine?" Make homemade play dough (recipe below). Put in zip lock bag with card that has message above written on it. Give to Sunday School classmates and friends.

Q

Color: Pink

Number: 6

Shape: Heart

Scripture: For if ye forgive men their trespasses, your heavenly Father will also forgive you. Matthew 6:14

Theme: **Quack Like a Duck**

Bible

- Scripture: For if ye forgive men their trespasses, your heavenly Father will also forgive you. Matthew 6:14
- Tell the story of Joseph and the Coat of Many Colors. Keep it simple. Joseph's father loved him and gave him a special coat made from many colors of fabric. His brothers were jealous. They sold Joseph as a slave and told their father an animal had killed him. Years later, Joseph became the King's official. His brothers came to see him. When they realized who he was they said they were sorry. Joseph forgave them. Joseph helped them have food to eat. He got to see his father and little brother again too. They came to live with him.
- Cut 2 coat shapes each from wallpaper sample books (usually the old ones will be given away free at places where wallpaper is sold); play a game of match with these colorful coats

Theme Learning

- Read, Make Way for Ducklings by Robert McCloskey; discuss what a duck looks like: webbed feet, water-proof feathers, beak or bill
- What do ducks eat? grasses, grains, water plants, fish, and insects
- Duck Flying Formation – ducks fly south where it is warmer in the winter; they fly in a V-shaped pattern and switch places; they fly this way to conserve energy…there is a reduction in wind resistance for those in the back; flying this way helps the group to fly longer without getting tired out; this pattern also helps them keep up with where everyone (fighter pilots also fly this way for that reason)
- Where do duck live? ducks live near wetlands, marshes, ponds, rivers, lakes and oceans; ducks live in nests near these water sources; their nest are usually made from sticks, grass, leaves, feathers,

Letter Skills

- Say It: Q says "q" like a quilt
- Practice It: Spread quilt on floor and tell child he may roll on quilt if he says "q" sound; repeat
- Recognize It: Decorate Blank Letter Q with small fabric squares to form a "quilt"
- Letter Q Box – fill empty wet-wipes box with small items that begin with letter Q (quarter, Q-tip, quilt square, toy queen, etc.)
- Q is for Q-tips – let children write letter Q's using Q-tips and paint

- Q like Quick game – let students take turns retrieving rubber ducks that have been placed around the room; instruct students they must move as quickly as they can and bring the duck back to the carpet
- Q is for Quack – Draw letter Q on construction paper; add another line to make the duck bill and add a wiggle eye

Math
- Fruit Loop Sorting-put the different color fruit loops onto that same color construction paper math mat
- Old Telephone Counting-give child old telephone or unplug an extra one you have and let him use for this activity; call out a number and have him try to find and push that number on the telephone
- Old Computer Keyboard-use as if telephone in above activity
- Pick Up Ducks game – write numbers 1-6 on the bottom of rubber ducks (or paper cut outs); add these ducks to a bucket filled with water; let children take turns picking up a duck, turning it over and calling out the number they see; put duck back in water; repeat until everyone has a turn
- 6 Seconds game – use a kitchen timer to show the kids how long 6 seconds is; them when you say go, they will do an action for 6 seconds until timer beeps (keep eyes closed; clap hands; nod head; quack like a duck; etc.)
- Number Flashcards – review numbers 1-6 using flashcards
- 6 Little Ducks song –
  6 little ducks went out to play
  Over the hills and far away
  Mother duck said, "Quack, Quack, Quack!"
  And all the little ducks came waddling back
  Repeat with 5 little ducks…4 little ducks…etc.

Shape Practice
- Candy Box Tracing -save old heart shaped candy box after Valentine's Day; let child trace around the shape

- Give child play dough with heart shaped cookie cutters
- Shape Duck-cut following shapes from construction paper and let child glue to form duck shape; large oval for body, small circle for head, 2 hearts for wings; can also add 2 orange stars for feet and orange diamond shape for beak

Color
- Pink Cotton Candy-purchase pink cotton candy from movie store and let your child "eat" the color pink; make him tell you what color he is eating with each bite
- Have child mix red and white paint to make pink
- Pink Pokey – create a pink streamer for each child by securing several strips of pink streamers to the end of a straw; sing the Pink Pokey and let children use their streams while singing

  Pink Pokey
  You put your pink in.
  You take your pink out,
  You put your pink in and you shake it all about
  Do the pink pokey and you turn yourself around.
  That's what it's all about.

Art
- Paint with feathers as you would a paintbrush
- Duckling Foot Prints-dip plastic fork in yellow paint and let child "walk" the fork across white paper to make duck chick's footprints
- Paper Plate Duck-fold yellow paper plate in half, colored side out and staple or tape together; trace child's hand on yellow construction paper and cut out; stick hand in back end of duck for feathers; straight part of folded plate should be up; glue yellow circle to head end and glue on orange beak

Music
- Play Lively Music and have child waddle and quack like a duck
- Egg Shakers-place Cheerios in plastic Easter eggs and use as shakers

Game Time
- Dunk the Ducks-add rubber ducks to large bucket of water (place vinyl, waterproof tablecloth underneath to help with spills); give child toy ball and let him try to dunk the ducks
- Play Duck, Duck, Goose with siblings or friends

Snack Idea
- Strawberry Milkshake-have child mix white milk and strawberry syrup and watch it turn pink as it is stirred

Fieldtrip Ideas
- Visit a local pond that has ducks; take bread to feed the ducks (be sure to supervise well around water)

- Watch the movie, "Charlotte's Web"
- Have a local farmer bring in a duck and maybe even ducklings for the children to see

R

Color: White
Number: 7
Shape: Diamond
Scripture: Be not overcome of evil, but overcome evil with good. Romans 12:21

Theme: **Reduce, Reuse, Recycle**

Bible

- Scripture: Be not overcome of evil, but overcome evil with good. Romans 12:21
- Tell the Story of Paul. Keep it simple. Saul was very mean to Christians. While on his way to Damascus, a bright light shown from heaven. Saul was blinded. Saul knew God wanted him to follow Him. Saul changed his name to Paul. After that, he spent the rest of his life telling about Jesus. He was shipwrecked, put in jail, beaten, and stoned, but kept telling others about Jesus.

Theme Learning

- What does reduce, reuse, recycle mean?
  Definitions:
  reduce - to use less
  reuse - to put again into service without changing
  recycle - to put again into service with changing
- What is a Recycling Center?
  A place where trash is separated into things that can/cannot be recycled…for example paper, plastic, aluminum, other metals, and wood
- What is a landfill?
  After reusable and recyclable materials have been removed at the Recycling Center, the remaining household waste is trucked here. Each evening, large trucks roll over the landfill to crush the day's garbage and then cover it with six inches of soil so the waste doesn't smell or attract flies and rats.
- What is Composting?
  Composting is when you make a pile of things such as grass clippings, leaves, and even food scraps; these things will decompose and can be added back to the soil to provide rich nutrients that plants need to grow healthy

Letter Skills

- Say It: R says "r" like motorcycle sound "rrrrrr"
- Practice It: Roll the ball and have child say "r" sound when he catches ball before he rolls it back
- Recognize It: Decorate Blank Letter R with rice

- Letter R box – fill empty wet wipes box with small things that start with R (rice, toy rabbit, toy railroad train, red crayon, toilet roll, recipe card, etc.)
- R is for Rainbow – write R on white paper; have child trace beside your r with another color and then another and another…continue until you have a rainbow R
- Find the R's – give each child a magazine page and have him circle or highlight all the r's; paste onto construction paper with title "R Hunt"
- R is for Red – if child can correctly say the "r" sound when asked what R says, he can come up and put a red dot circle sticker on you (you will look like you have the chicken pox, but the kids will really enjoy this)

Math
- Birthday Cake Candle Counting-purchase Styrofoam flat circle that looks like cake shape; provide child with birthday candles and let him add 7 candles to the cake; he will enjoy putting them in and out (for Circle Time, pass out candles and let children come up and put candle in as you count; count backwards and remove them; repeat
- Cereal Box Puzzles-cut the colorful front from a cereal box into pieces for an instant puzzle
- Easter Egg Counting-put 12 eggs into clean egg carton; use permanent marker to write numbers on egg and inside egg carton cup; have child count and place number of Cheerios cereal pieces into each egg; match correct egg with cup
- Recycled Wind Chime – Let children help count aloud as you hold up 7 baby food jar lids (pre-drill holes) and string to wire clothes hanger; hang outside on tree for recycled wind chime; can also recycle old silverware using same idea
- Recycling Saves Money – count money…1 through 7 pennies; pass pennies out to 7 children and let them come up one at a time and drop into a piggy bank as you count; get them out and have 7 more children come up; repeat until everyone has had a turn

Shape Practice
- I Spy a Diamond-cut and hang diamonds around the house; give child flashlight and let him hunt for octagons; shine light on shape when he finds it
- Diamond Tangrams-cut diamond shapes from fun foam; let children put the diamond shapes together to make new shapes or to make pictures

Color:
- Give child black construction paper and white chalk; let him make a white chalk picture
- Point out color of white milk at next snack
- White Pencil Can-let toddler paint a clean soup can using white paint; when dry let child add stickers, glitter, etc. to decorate pencil can
- Make a list of all of the white things the children can think of (milk, chalk, clouds, paper, teeth, etc.)
- Color Flashcards – pull out construction paper sheets in the colors that you have already learned; show each color and let children tell you what color it is

Art:
- Recycled Sock Hand Puppet-dip child's old tube sock in water that has been tinted with green food coloring in water; pin to clothes line and let it dry; hot glue on two wiggle eyes and piece of red felt for mouth; child size sock is perfect for their hand and they will have fun wearing this snake puppet
- Recycled Lid Bird Feeder-use plastic lid from oatmeal, coffee, etc.; punch holes and add yarn for hanging; add birdseed or stale bread
- Recycle Old Christmas Cards-cut cards into puzzles and store in zip lock bags
- Recycle Old Crayons-place broken crayons in lightly greased mini muffin tin, melt at 250 degrees and pop out when cool

Music:
- Recycled Kazoo-collect old paper towel roll and put a wax paper circle on the end (cut larger than the end); secure with rubber band for instant kazoo
- Pots and Pan Band-Reuse pots and pans as drums; wooden spoons can be the drum sticks
- Recycled Stuffed Animal Puppet-pick old stuffed animal such as a teddy bear; cut hole in bottom which will be the hole where child's hand will go; remove stuffing from body part of bear; leave stuffing in head and bottom legs; remove stuffing from top arms so child's fingers can fit in; cute and free puppet; have a puppet show

Game Time:
- Pick up the Trash Game-ball up white scrap paper or old newspaper and throw all over the ground; give child laundry basket and let them pick up trash; dump basket out and keep going
- Homemade Bubbles-make bubbles from dish detergent and find household items to reuse as bubble wands; try fly swatter, end of toilet roll, straw, berry basket etc.
- Soda Bottle Bowling-reuse empty soda bottles and set up like bowling pins; use toy ball to bowl and try to knock down pins
- Label large laundry baskets and have children help sort items used this week that could be recycled; examples: "plastics basket" for milk jug and soda bottles; "aluminum basket" for soda cans; "tin basket" for tin cans; basket for grocery store plastic sacks, etc.
- Recycle Refrigerator Box-call local appliance store and ask them if they will save it for you; cut door in it and let child use it as a play house; take off top and bottom and it's an instant tunnel; the possibilities are endless and this will be a sure favorite (Extra Idea: use large foam paintbrush to brush on sand; sprinkle sand all over box to make a sand castle

Snack Idea:
- Eat donut holes; discuss how they are the part of the donut that is often discarded
- Painted Bread-color milk with food coloring; give child clean paint brush and let him paint the bread; toast these for a colorful snack; tell them recycling is good for the earth so maybe they want to paint grass, flowers, tree, etc.

- Earth Cupcake – give each child a cupcake that has been frosted with white frosting; let them each add a drop of blue gel food coloring and a drop of green gel food coloring; move the gel around with a clean popsicle stick to look like the earth
- Recycle colorful magazine pages as place mats for snack time

Fieldtrip Ideas
- Visit your local Recycling Center
- Watch movie, "A Bug's Live" (they use reuse many items such as a leaf and water droplet telescope)

S

Color: White

Number: 7

Shape: Diamond

Scripture: The hearing ear, and the seeing eye, the LORD hath made even both of them.

Proverbs 20:12

Theme: **Senses (My Five Senses)**

Bible
- Scripture: The hearing ear, and the seeing eye, the LORD hath made even both of them. Proverbs 20:12
- Tell the story of Jesus at the Temple. Every year Jesus' parents went to Jerusalem for the Passover Festival. When Jesus was 12 years old, after the festival he stayed behind to talk to the church teachers. For three days, Mary and Joseph couldn't find Jesus. They found Him in the temple. The teachers were amazed at how much He knew about God. He knew because He is God's Son.
- Stained Glass Church Window-glue tissue paper squares to piece of plastic (like overhead transparency); cut out church window shape from black construction paper and glue on top of tissue squares

Theme Learning
- Intro. The 5 Senses: Sight, Hearing, Touch, Smell, Taste; let children point to the part of their body used for each sense
- Mystery Touch Box - tape an empty shoebox closed; cut a hole in one of the long ends-big enough for a child's arm to fit in; decorate with colorful contact paper, if you'd like; place an item inside and pass the box telling children to feel what's inside, but not to tell what they think it is; when everyone has had a turn, let them all say together what they thought the item was; repeat with other items
- Taste Test-provide sweet, sour, salty and bitter things to taste; examples are: sugar, lemon, potato chip; cocoa
- Hide and Seek Whistle – move to a location in the room and blow a whistle and let children close eyes and point in the direction they hear the whistle; repeat from different locations

Letter Skills
- Say It: S says "s" like a snake
- Play a Game: Have toddler pretend to be snake as he makes the "s" sound; call on one child at a time
- Recognize It: Decorate Blank Letter S by gluing on small pieces of string (yarn)
- S is for Sight Collage – draw two eyes in the center of a piece of construction paper; have child cut out pictures from magazines that their eyes help them see and past around the eyes on the construction paper (Note: This page will be added to My 5 Senses Book - sight)

- S is for Sound – draw a bell shape from yellow construction paper and cut out; have child glue that bell to another piece of construction paper; add a popsicle stick for handle; explain that we can hear a bell ring because of our sense of hearing (Note: This page will be added to My 5 Senses Book – hearing)
- S is for Smelly Flower – have child glue cupcake liner to construction paper; draw a green stem and leaves; spray a cotton ball with perfume and have child glue to middle of cupcake liner flower; write smelly flower at the bottom of the page and let child circle the letter s
- Hot Snake (like Hot Potato) – make a simple sock snake using tube sock stuffed with fiberfill pillow stuffing and hot glue to close; add wiggle eyes and a red felt tongue; use markers to decorate; have children toss (or pass) the snake and say the "s" sound when they are holding snake

Math
- Counting Sheep Game-write numbers 1-7 on pieces of paper and lay in line on floor; place a soft pillow at the end; have child count and crawl from number to number until he reaches the pillow where he can pretend to sleep
- Puzzles-wooden puzzles with peg on top of each pieces are a great toddler activity
- M&M Counting - Collect old plastic lids/tops such as from shaving crème; write numbers 1-7 on each; give child M&M's and have him put that number of candy in each top (can use small paper cups as well)
- Number 7 Stomp – Show number flashcards and instruct students that when they see number 7, they should stand and stomp seven times
- 7 Silly Snakes rhyme/fingerplay – hold fingers up as you say the following:
  7 Silly Snakes (like 5 Little Ducks)
  7 silly snakes went out to play,
  Over the hills and far away.
  Mother snake said, "sss-sss-sss"
  And 7 silly snakes came slithering back.
  --Repeat with 6, 5, 4…no silly snakes--

Shape Practice
- Diamond Stamping-cut corners from rectangular sponge to make a diamond shape; pour paint on paper plate or in disposable pie pan; dip and paint
- Diamond like a Square – make a diamond shape by taping straws together; show the children that if you push on the diamond shaped straws   , it becomes a square; discuss how diamonds and squares are alike (4 equal sides, 4 corners)
- Diamond Mining – explain that real diamonds are mined (dirt and rock is hammered away to reveal the diamond…usually in underground caves); hold up various shapes (use flashcards) and tell children to pretend to hammer when they see you hold up a diamond shape

Color
- Make homemade play dough; don't add food coloring and it will remain white; as child plays with it discuss how it feels (smooth, cool)

- o Homemade Play dough
  1 cup flour
  2 teaspoons cream of tartar (spice section)
  ½ tsp salt, 1 cup water
  1 tbsp vegetable oil
  Cook in saucepan over medium heat, stirring constantly until forms a ball; remove, cool, and knead
- Saint Patrick handprint-paint four fingers white (for beard); paint palm pink (for face); paint top of hand and thumb green (for hat); press hand down and add eyes and mouth with marker
- White snake – provide white tube sock and have child stuff with fiber fill or old pillow stuffing; secure end by sewing or using hot glue; use marker to draw eyes and forked tongue; use this stuffed snake to reinforce "s" sound during Letter Skills time
- Look for White – remind children that we use our eyes to help us see; look around and let each child name something around him that is white…try to find something that no one else has mentioned
- White Cottonball – give each child a cotton ball; let him/her feel how soft it is; tell them to rub it against their face; talk about the color white

Art

- Hand Collage-cut out large hand print and have child glue on cotton ball, sandpaper, textured fabric, piece of lace, etc.; discuss sense of touch (Note: This page will be added to My 5 Senses Book - touch)
- Gingerbread Man-cut gingerbread man shape from brown construction paper; let child glue to another piece of construction paper, add glue for eyes, mouth, buttons, etc. and sprinkle with cinnamon; discuss sense of smell (Note: This page will be added to My 5 Senses Book - smell)
- Binoculars-use toilet tubs taped together for binoculars; have child decorate; discuss sense of sight
- Beet Painting-draw a picture of a tongue on white construction paper; use beet juice poured from can of beets to paint with; makes a nice dark pink color; let child taste a beet and discuss sense of taste (Note: This page will be added to My 5 Senses Book - taste)

Music

- Musical Instruments-collect all of the instruments you have; arrange student chairs in a big circle; place one instrument on each chair; each child stands by a chair and plays that instrument until you say, "Switch." Each child moves to the next chair until everyone has had a turn to play every instrument (make instruments if you don't have enough…for example two spoons tapped together, pots and pans, jingle bells, etc.
- Sing "Oh Be Careful Little Eyes What You See…" use eyes/see; nose/smell; tongue/taste; hands/feel

Game Time
- Play "I Spy"
- What's in the Sack Game-have different things in a brown paper sack and have child feel and guess what each things is
- Hide and Seek with Whistle-tell children to close their eyes; you will hide and blow a whistle; have them listen to whistle sound to know where to find you; (For Circle Time, they should stay seated, but just point in the direction they hear the whistle.)
- Guess the Sound – in advance walk around the center and even around town and make a recording of sounds that the children are likely to hear (dog barking, typing on computer, tea kettle whistling, adults talking, feet walking, etc.); play the recording and students try to guess what they are hearing

Snack Idea
- Handprint Sugar Cookies-roll out store bought dough and use handprint cookie cutter
- Jello Jigglers - use handprint cookie cutter, if you'd like

Fieldtrip Ideas
- Visit bakery – discuss the sense of taste; usually bakeries will let each child decorate a cookie

Note: There are 5 pages that can be stapled together to create a My 5 Senses Book to go home on Friday.

T
Color: White
Number: 7
Shape: Diamond
Scripture: …Suffer the little children to come unto me... Mark 10:14

Theme: **Terrific Teeth**

Bible

- Scripture: …Suffer the little children to come unto me… Mark 10:14
- Tell the story of Jesus and the Children. Keep it simple. One day Jesus was teaching. A group of mothers wanted their children to meet Jesus. They brought the children to him, but the disciples said, "No." Jesus saw what happened and told the disciples to let the children come to Him. He took the children up into his arms, laid His hands on them and blessed them.
- Sing: "Jesus Loves the Little Children"

Theme Learning

- Intro. Teeth theme – What are teeth made of?
  Teeth are made up of four main parts. On the outside is a protective layer of enamel - the hardest substance in the body. Below that is a bone-like substance called dentin, which makes up the largest part of the tooth. Underneath the dentin, the tooth actually has a soft center. This is called the pulp, and it houses all of the tooth's blood vessels and nerve endings. Finally, the cementum covers the roots. Copied from www.aquafresh.com
- How can I take care of my teeth? Brush 2 times a day, floss your teeth, stay away from too many sugary foods, visit the dentist twice a year, drink milk, raw foods like apples help clean the teeth
- Colorful Stained Teeth-cut tooth shape from white construction paper; glue tooth to another full sheet of construction paper and cover entire page with clear contact paper; discuss with child that when you eat sweet things your teeth get dirty and need to be cleaned. Color part of tooth with water base purple marker to resemble grape jelly…color part of tooth with red marker to resemble red sucker..continue with other colors; have child clean tooth with damp rag; water base markers will clean easily (test before doing activity) Note: Each child will make one of these during Center Time
- How many teeth do I have? Preschoolers have 20..adults have 32. Discuss baby teeth versus permanent teeth. Explain that between the ages of 6 to 12, children lose their teeth and those are replaced with permanent ones.

Letter Skills

- Say It: T says "t" like a ticking clock
- Play a Game: while you pretend to be asleep, have children pretend to be clocks and make the "t" ticking sound; have one child ring a bell to signify alarm clock ringing and then you "wake up"; repeat allowing everyone a chance to ring the bell

- Recognize It: Decorate Blank Letter T with torn bits of colorful paper
- Letter T box – fill empty wet wipes box with small items that begin with letter T (timer, toy turtle, tooth, top, telephone-old cell phone, etc.)
- Pulling Teeth game – cut a simple mouth shape from red construction paper; tape on white squares for teeth (note-roll the tape and add to back of tooth to attach to mouth); be sure there is one tooth for each child in the class; if child can say the "t" sound correctly when asked what T says, he had come up and "pull" one tooth out by taking it off the poster
- T is for Train Tracks – cut out two trips from brown construction paper; have child draw lines up and down and across so that each strip looks like a set of train tracks; Glue the strips to another piece of paper to look letter T
- T is for Toothbrush – cut toothbrush shape from construction paper; have child add pieces of yarn for the bristles; glue to another piece of construction paper; write T is for toothbrush at the bottom and have child circle the t's

Math

- Kangaroo Counting-give child an apron (like the kind at Home Stores used for holding tools); write numbers 1-7 on index card; have child hop to number try to tell what it is and put it in his pouch (apron)
- Bank-Use old can with lid (such as Pringles can) and cut slit in top to make a homemade bank; since coins are choking hazards, purchase larger Poker chips and let your child put these "coins" into the bank (a sure favorite great for fine motor skills)
- Counting Teeth-use mini marshmallows which look like teeth to count 1-7
- Repeat the Pattern – chomp teeth together 7 times, clap 7 times, tap fingers 7 times, blink 7 times, etc.)
- Number Flashcard Review – show various flashcards and instruct children that when they see number 7 they should pretend to brush teeth

Shape Practice

- Crown Jewels-run through Burger King drive through and ask for a paper crown; have child glue diamond shaped craft jewels onto the crown; you could also cut crown shapes from colorful fun foam or construction paper
- Potato Print-cut potato in half and use knife to cut away a diamond shape; dip in paint and stamp
- Walk Around the Diamond – use blue painters tape to create a large diamond shape on the floor; children should line up and walk around the diamond shape

Color

- Magnetic Color Practice-give child cookie sheet and magnetic letters; have him find color you call out and place on cookie sheet; magnets will stick on metal pan
- White Cotton Ball collecting-use kitchen tongs to move white cotton balls from one bucket to another
- Colorful Stained Teeth-cut tooth shape from white construction paper; glue tooth to another full sheet of construction paper and cover entire page with clear contact

paper; discuss with child that when you eat sweet things your teeth get dirty and need to be cleaned. Color part of tooth with water base purple marker to resemble grape jelly…color part of tooth with red marker to resemble red sucker..continue with other colors; have child clean tooth with damp rag; water base markers will clean easily (test before doing activity)

- I Spy White – look around for things that are white in the room; let each child have a turn to spot something
- ToothFairy, ToothFairy, Who Has Your Tooth? (like Doggy, Doggy, Where's Your Bone) one student sits in chair facing away from class, place paper tooth cutout under chair; point to one child who quietly sneaks up and takes tooth and hides in lap; the Tooth Fairy has 3 guesses to discover who took the tooth

Art

- Alligator Teeth Painting-cut egg cartons in half and give each child row of 6 alligator teeth; use paint brush to paint the alligator's teeth white (this only works with the cardboard type egg cartons versus the shiny type…have parents save in advance)
- Paint with toothbrush – provide toothbrushes to use as paintbrushes and let children paint on a white piece of paper
- Tooth Fairy Bag – cut two, C-shaped pieces of felt for each child; punch holes along the sides and let child use yarn to lace up around the shape; put knots in the ends; glue white felt tooth shape to the front of bag

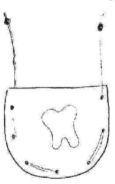

Music

- Baby Bottle Shakers-recycle those old, clear plastic baby bottles by filling with rice, beans, etc.; secure the top with masking tape for instant shakers; for added fun buy colorful Nerds candies and pour inside; these are fun to look at (can use baby food jar…just be careful about breakage) Explain that baby's shouldn't go to sleep with a baby bottle…it's bad for their teeth.
- Train Follow the Leader – play music and have children make a train, one behind the other, moving all around the room; change train engine and caboose often so that everyone gets a turn

Game Time

- Feed the Monster-draw a fun looking monster with teeth on large poster board and secure to back of kitchen chair; cut a large mouth into the board; give child pieces of paper that has been balled up and let him try to toss the monster food into the monster's mouth
- Soda Bottle Bowling-discuss that soda isn't good for teeth, but make a great game; use the empty bottles from a recycling center set up like bowling pins; use ball to try and knock down all the pins (Explain that soda is not good for your teeth.)

Snack Idea
- Mini Marshmallows-look like teeth and make a great snack; add stick pretzel toothbrushes if you'd like (if there are no peanut allergies in your class, take an apple slice and spread with peanut butter and then top with mini marshmallow teeth and another slice of apple on top for a cute smile)

Fieldtrip Ideas
- Visit the dentist's office
- Have a hygienist come in to speak with the class
- Watch show, "Arthur's Tooth" (on PBS by author Marc Brown)

Special Holiday Week
Letter: Review
Color: White
Number: Review
Shape: Diamond

Scripture: For all have sinned, and come short of the glory of God. Romans 3:23

Theme: **Easter Week**

Bible
- Scripture: For all have sinned, and come short of the glory of God. Romans 3:23
- Tell Easter Story. Keep it simple: Homemade Resurrection Eggs-save and wash a half dozen egg carton; write numbers 1-6 inside each egg cup; write corresponding numbers on plastic Easter eggs; put the following items in each and use to tell the Easter story:
  - #1 leaf (When Jesus entered Jerusalem, people waved palm leaves)
  - #2 Cheerio (Jesus ate the "Last Supper" with his friends)
  - #3 purple cloth (a purple robe was put on Jesus)
  - #4 nail (Jesus was nailed to the cross & took the punishment for our sins)
  - #5 cotton ball sprayed with perfume (spices used to prepare His body)
  - #6 leave empty (Jesus was not in the tomb, He arose.)

Theme Learning
- Triumphal Entry – Jesus rode into Jerusalem on a donkey; people took off their coats and put them on the ground for Jesus to ride on top of; they waved palm branches and shouted, "Hosanna," which is a word people used to show praise and joy; give each child a "palm branch" you cut from green construction paper; let them wave the branch and sing, "Praise Him, Praise Him, All Ye Little Children…" or another praise song
- The Last Supper – Jesus and his disciples met to eat together; Jesus said the bread was to remind us of His body which He gave for us…the juice was to remind us of His blood which he shed on the cross for us. After supper, Jesus washed the disciples feet to show them that they should serve others (have the children take off socks and shoes and "wash" their feet with a wet wipe)
- Praying in the Garden – Judas (one of Jesus' disciples) told soldiers where to find Jesus. He was praying in a garden. Peter didn't want them to take Jesus. He took his sword and cut off one of the soldier's ears. Jesus healed the soldier's ear. He knew that this was God's plan. The soldiers took Jesus.
- Crucifixion and Resurrection – Jesus was crucified on a cross. This was God's plan because the punishment for sin (the bad things we do) is death. Jesus took our punishment. Jesus was buried in a tomb (like a cave). A big stone was placed in front of the tomb. Three days later, Jesus rose from the grave. Two ladies both named Mary came to see the tomb. They saw an angel sitting on the stone. The angel had moved the stone to show that no one was there. The angel said, "He is not here: for He is risen, as He said."

Letter Skills
- Review Letters covered so far
- Review all letter boxes A – T (each week, fill empty wet wipes containers with things that begin with the letter of the week…you will have 26 boxes at the end of the year)
- Sing the Alphabet Song to review all letters
- Erase the letter – write letters learned so far on the board (A-T); have student come up and erase the letter you say; repeat so that everyone has a turn
- Pick a Pocket game – purchase one of those hanging shoe organizers with lots of pockets; put a letter in each (cut out from paper or use ABC magnets); children take turns coming up and pulling letter from pocket – he should tell what letter it is and what sound it makes
- Trace magnetic alphabet letters
- Alphabet stamping – purchase a set of ABC stamps and stamp pad and let the children stamp the letters on white paper
- Play dough with alphabet cookie cutters
- Sing: What's the Sound song to review all letters
  What's the Sound – tune B-I-N-G-O
  What's the sound that starts these words
  _____ and _____ and _____
  / / is the sound, / / is the sound, / / is the sound
  That starts _____, _____, and _____.

Math
- Review Numbers covered so far
- Flashlight Writing – turn off the lights and use a flashlight to "write" a number on the wall or ceiling; children must try to guess what number you wrote
- Who Has # __ ? game – give each child an index card that has a number on it; call out a number and those children who have it should stand; repeat several times and then let the children switch numbers with their neighbor
- Fishing for Numbers – provide a stick with yarn tied on one end; hot glue a magnet to the other end of the yarn; cut out fish shapes and add large metal gem clip at mouth; let children take turns fishing for the number you call out…or have them pull out a fish and tell you what number it is
- What Comes After game – call out a number and have children try to tell what number comes next…before

Shape Practice
- Diamond Hide and Seek: Hide diamond cutouts all over the house and let your toddler go on a diamond hunt.
- Diamond Stamping-cut diamond shape from inexpensive sponge and let child stamp away

Color
- Play with white play dough.
- Finger paint with white paint on black paper.

- Easter Egg Color Hunt: fill large rubber maid container with several bags of Easter grass (or paper from shredder); hid plastic eggs inside; as child finds egg, have him tell you the color
- Colorful Easter Table Cloth-purchase inexpensive twin size white sheet (or use old sheet); use clothespins to affix sheet to fencer or just lay on ground outside; fill several spray bottles with different colors of fabric paint; let child spray the paint all over the sheet; when dry these make colorful table clothes for the kid's table during Easter dinner

Art

- Make Resurrection Eggs – see Bible section for more details; use half dozen size egg carton for each child (see Resources section for label and copies of little papers that go inside each egg explaining what each thing means)
- Easter Bucket-ask large restaurant like Cracker Barrel or a local public school to save a big vegetable can for you; wash out and spray paint white; let child add stickers, paint, fun foam Easter shapes, glitter, etc. to decorate; drill two holes in each side and string ribbon in holes for handle; put Easter grass in bottom
- "Dye" Easter Eggs-explain that the reason we "dye" them is to remember that Jesus "died" for us
- Decoupage Eggs-provide plastic Easter eggs; seasonal printed, brightly colored napkins; and watered down glue with paint brush; let child tear the napkins into small pieces; paint the egg with glue and stick napkin pieces on top; when covered, brush with glue all over to smooth down any loose ends; when dry, place in a basket and these will be a lovely table decoration
- Plant A Basket Full of Flowers-recycle old Easter basket by adding plastic to bottom for liner (large zip lock works well); add soil and seeds; attach a bow to handle; this makes a great Easter gift for grandparents

Music

- Jelly Bean Shaker-jelly beans are a choking hazard for young children, but they make great, colorful shakers; put jelly beans in clean water bottle; secure lid and shake away; toddlers will love looking at all the bright colored jelly beans shaking around
- Sing, "We Wish You a Happy Easter" as you would "We Wish You a Merry Christmas"
- Sing, "Happy Easter to You" (like Happy Birthday) – Happy Easter to you…Happy Easter to you…Happy Easter dear friends…Happy Easter to you
- Do the Bunny Pokey-put your ears, nose, cotton tail, feet, etc. in

Game Time

- Easter Egg Hunt-explain that eggs are a sign of new life in Spring
- Bunny Hop Relay-have starting line and finish line and let children hop instead of run
- Pin Tail on Bunny-provide bunny outline and cotton ball for tail; invite friends over for this (focus should not be on Easter bunny; instead tell children that baby bunnies are born this time of year; Easter means new life)

Snack Idea

- Cross Shaped Jell-O Jigglers-make Jell-O Jigglers according to package directions; use cross shaped cookie cutter to cut
- Resurrection Rolls-unroll crescent rolls on baking sheet; take large marshmallow and roll in butter and then in cinnamon; place one in middle of each crescent roll and have child wrap crescent roll securely around the marshmallow; pinch any holes shut; bake according to crescent roll package directions (approx. 350 for 10 min.); marshmallow will melt leaving an empty "tomb;" these are meaningful and delicious (See next page for step by step photos)

Fieldtrip Ideas

- Easter Egg Hunt outside

Resurrection Rolls

Step 1

Step 2

Step 3

U

Color: Black

Number: 8

Shape: Octagon (stop sign)

Scripture: I do set my bow in the cloud, and it shall be for a token of a covenant between me and the earth. Genesis 9:13

Theme: **Umbrellas, Spring Showers, and Other Signs of Spring**

Bible
- Scripture: I do set my bow in the cloud, and it shall be for a token of a covenant between me and the earth. Genesis 9:13
- Tell story of Noah. Keep it simple. Long ago, people were not obeying God. One man named Noah did obey God. God told Noah that He would send a flood. He told Noah to build a big boat. God sent two of each kind of animal into the ark and seven of certain animals. God shut the door and the rain came down for forty days and nights. Finally, the boat set down on land. Noah got out and built an alter and thanked God. God sent a rainbow as a promise that He would not send another flood to destroy the Earth.
- Cereal Rainbow: glue colorful Fruitloops cereal on construction paper to make a rainbow.

Theme Learning
- Discuss Signs of Spring – grass grows quickly, flowers blooming, tree buds, nests in trees, baby animals born…
- Discuss Weather in Spring – windy, rainy (use hairdryer to discuss wind; use umbrella to discuss rain)
- What Makes the Rain – water that is on the ground evaporates (warms up and turns into gas and rises up into the sky); the gas cools down in the sky and turns back into water droplets; water droplets clump together and when there are enough they fall back down as rain
- Spring Planting – farmers begin planting their gardens once the weather is warm enough; they plant cucumbers, tomatoes, peppers, watermelons, etc. Briefly review how to plant and what plants need to grow

Letter Skills
- Say It: U says "u" like when you have been poked in stomach with finger
- Play a Game: let child gently poke belly as he says "u" sound when asked
- Recognize It: Decorate Blank Letter U with fingerprint raindrops; just dip child's finger into blue paint; let him glue on a cotton ball cloud above the U.
- Letter U box – fill empty wet wipes box with small things that begin with U (umbrella-like you would put in a drink; unzip-cut zipper from old jeans, utensil, arrow pointing up, etc.)
- Letter U Water Color Painting – Let children use water color paints to paint U's on white paper

- U Macaroni Picture – Write letter U on construction paper using thick, black marker; let children trace the letter U with glue and then glue elbow macaroni (which looks like u's) to it

Math
- Count the Flowers-provide 8 single artificial flowers for your child to count
- Straw Counters-explain that plants use roots that act like straws so that they can drink in water and grow; use straws for counters; count 1-8 using straws
- Flower Stickers – write #7 at the top and have children put 7 flower stickers on paper, they can decorate their pictures by drawing grass, trees, sun, clouds, etc.
- In My Garden – Write In My Garden, I would plant _____ at the bottom of a sheet of paper; make copies for everyone; have children dictate to you what they would want to plant in their Spring garden; have them color brown dirt and glue on 8 seeds (any variety..could even use beans)
- 8 Blades of Grass – have child glue 8 pieces of string to green construction paper; write the heading: 8 Blades of Grass

Shape Practice
- Trace the Shape-draw outline of octagon on paper; let child glue Cheerios on the shape outline
- Spaghetti Noodle Shapes-boil long spaghetti noodles, form in shape of octagon, shape will harden when dry
- Look at Stop Signs-next time you go on fieldtrip have the children point out all the stop signs they see; reinforce octagon shape

Color
- Black Cloud-discuss how black (dark) clouds are a sign that rain is coming; use black finger paint to make black storm clouds
- Color Song-Sing this song as you would "Brown Bear, Brown Bear, What do you see" except you sing the words, "Color Red, Color Red, What do you see?" You will hold up construction paper in the next color and sing, "I see Color Orange looking at me." Continue with all the colors learned so far.

Art
- Coffee Filter Umbrella-use water color paint set to paint coffee filter; the colors will be pretty and pastel; when dry attach center to a straw to resemble an umbrella
- Cupcake Liner Flowers-glue cupcake liner bottom to paper for flower; add greed stem and leaves; add cotton ball cloud, if desired
- Spring Wind Sock-cut end off of paper lunch sack, decorate sack using markers, glitter, etc.; tape colorful streamers to the end and hang outside using yarn
- Spring Binoculars – make binoculars by stapling two toilet rolls together; let children decorate with Spring stickers; punch holes on sides and add yarn neck strap (use on Nature Walk during Game Time)

Music
- Umbrella Dancing-children love to play with umbrellas; use a child size, safe umbrella and let your child dance to music; for added instruction give child directions as to how to hold the umbrella: up, down, right, left, behind back, in front, etc.
- Sing, "Rain, Rain, Go Away"
- Sing, "If all the raindrops were…" using letter sounds. For example, "If all the raindrops were letter A's, letter A's, Oh what a rain that would be. Standing outside with my mouth open wide. A-A-A-A-A-A-A-A-A-A (make letter a sounds)…" Great letter sound practice!

Game Time
- Puddle Jumping-spread small hand towels all around the room; tell children these are puddles made after a Spring rain; have them jump around the puddles and then from puddle to puddle, etc.
- Rain is Falling Down Game-cut raindrops from blue construction paper; sing, "Rain is falling down, won't you try and catch it. Rain is falling down, won't you try and catch it. Rain is falling down, won't you try and catch it. Catch it if you can."
- Go outside and plant a garden-a GREAT idea would be to plant pumpkin seeds now; they will be ready when October comes around
- Baby Chick Hatches Game-have child roll up in ball and place white men's t-shirt on them to represent the egg; when you tell them have them "hatch" out of the egg by stretching up and getting out of the t-shirt; discuss that usually baby animals are born in Spring
- Nature Walk – go outside and look for signs of Spring

Snack Idea
- Serve blue Jell-O with white Cool Whip-to represent blue sky and white clouds
- Fruity Pebble Rainbow Treats-use Fruity Pebbles Cereal as you would Rice Krispies to make these treats; make them in the same way you would the Rice Krispy Squares by melting the marshmallows and stirring in the cereal; press into muffin tins; these will be so colorful and yummy

Fieldtrip Ideas
- Visit a farm – hopefully there will be some baby animals to see and hold
- Visit the Feed and Seed – they will usually have baby chicks around this time of year
- Have a farmer come in and bring baby chicks for the children to hold
- Visit a flower nursery
- Have florist come in

V

Color: Black
Number: 8
Shape: Octagon (stop sign)
Scripture: Jesus saith unto him, I am the way, the truth, and the life: no man cometh unto the Father, but by Me. John 14:6

Theme: **Vroom, Vroom, Things That Go**

Bible:
- Scripture: Jesus saith unto him, I am the way, the truth, and the life: no man cometh unto the Father, but by Me. John 14:6
- Tell the story of The Tower of Babel. Keep it simple: A long time ago, people all spoke the same language. After the flood of Noah's time, God told the people to spread out across the land. They did not obey. They stayed together in one city. They began to build a tall tower, which they hoped would reach heaven. God caused them to begin to speak different languages. They had to obey God and spread out.
- Build tower with Lego's or blocks

Theme Learning
- Modes of transportation – land vehicles (cars, trucks, vans, taxi's, diesel trucks, dump trucks, trains...)
- Modes of transportation – air (planes, helicopters, hot air balloons, blimps...)
- Modes of transportation – water (boats, ships, sailboats, cargo ships, cruise ships...)
- Modes of transportation – outer space (rocket ships, space shuttles, lunar excursion modules, moon rover, Mars rover)

Letter Skills:
- Say It: V says "v" like "vroom"
- Play a Game: Draw a two-lane road on white poster board; divide the road into sections; divide class into two teams; let one child from each team place toy car at one end of the road; if child can tell you the "v" sound, he may move his team's car one space; continue asking, "What does V say?" If child answers without help, he can move forward; if he needs help, he must move back one space
- Recognize It: Decorate Blank Letter V with car tracks; put black paint in paper plate; run Hot Wheels cars through paint and have children roll on their letter U
- Letter V box – fill empty wet wipes box with small items that begin with letter V (picture of violin, small plastic vase, toy vegetables, etc.)
- V is for Vegetables – cut our pictures of vegetables from sale flyers; glue to construction paper; write heading V is for Vegetables; let child circle letter v's
- V Vroom game – show letter flashcards and when children see V they should all say Vroom! Vroom!; keep sticking letter V back into the deck, so there will be lots of opportunities to identify letter V

- Letter V Map – cut letter V shape from old map; glue to construction paper
- V is for Vase – cut 2 triangular shapes for each child from construction paper; write letter V on the triangle; let child help staple the sides closed; add an artificial flower

Math:

- Tanker Truck Wheel Counting-cut out large tanker truck shape from construction paper; have child use old milk jug caps and count and place 8 "wheels" on the truck
- Use large paintbrush and bucket of water to paint number 1's on sidewalk. Your toddlers will be amazed as the sun causes the number 1 to evaporate and disappear!
- Make violin cutout from construction paper; have child glue on 8 pieces of yarn for the stings
- Count 8 Cars – hot glue magnet to bottoms of 8 toy Hot Wheels Cars; provide a cookie pan; have children come up and stick a car to the pan as the class counts; count backwards to remove and give car to someone else; repeat
- 8 Planets sheet – have child trace 8 circles (use various sized tops-like milk jug cap, water bottle top, Pringles can lid, etc.); write heading 8 Planets at the top of the page [Explain to the children that there are 8 planets in our Solar System and three dwarf planets-Ceres, Pluto and Eris.]`
- Count 8 Keys – count together or pass out and have one child say number and bring key to you; repeat until everyone has had a turn
- 8 Wheels – dip the end of an empty spool of thread into black paint and stamp 8 wheels on a piece of white paper
- Train Whistle Counting – blow a wooden train whistle and have children tell you how many times the whistle blew (toot, toot = 2…toot-toot-toot-toot = 4…); use the numbers 1-8
- Roll the Planet Counting – roll a ball (planet) and tell child to call out next number if the ball is rolled to him; count/roll 8 times; repeat until everyone has had a turn; child should roll it back to you between each number

Shape Practice:
- Fun Foam Shape Magnets-cut shapes from fun foam; attach magnet to back and let child play with these shapes by placing them on cookie sheet
- Stop Sign game-cut red octagon from construction paper; let child jump, run in place etc. until you hold up sign and he must stop

Color:
- License Plate-cut black construction paper in half and let child use white chalk to design a license plate
- I Spy Black – children should look around and find things that are the color black (hands on the clock, letters on the rule poster, etc.)
- Review colors using paper airplanes made from construction paper

Art:
- School Bus Collage-cut yellow school bus shape from construction paper; find and cut pictures of children from magazine; glue in windows of bus
- Paper Airplanes-make and decorate paper airplanes
- Paper Plate Boat – place a small amount of play dough in center of a wax-coated paper plate; add a paper flag taped to Popsicle stick; instruct children to take home and sail in the bathtub
- Crayon Rubbing of License Plate – try to find one that has number 8 on it

Music:
- Freeze-cut green, yellow and red circles from construction paper; tape to Popsicle sticks; play lively music, hold up green circle when child can dance; hold up yellow circle and he must dance slowly, hold up red circle and he must freeze
- Sing "The Wheels on the Bus"-use different vehicles such as the "wheels on the train go chug, chug, chug…"

Game Time:
- Road Map-draw a road and other favorite spots such as church, the library, and favorite restaurant onto a large piece of poster board; let child use small toy cars to drive all around town
- Red Light/Green Light-have children get on one end of room or playground and when you hold up green circle they may run toward you; they must stop when you hold up red or they will have to go all the way back
- Ramp Fun-make ramps out of anything flat; the lid to a plastic storage box with books underneath one end will work well; let children put small toy cars at top of ramp and let go to watch them roll down (Great for Building Center)
- Boat Play-provide a large container filled with water and toy boats
- Bus Play-line up chairs, which will be the bus; children will love moving from drivers seat to other seats on the bus

- Pack Your Bags-let children use one of your suitcases and pack up bag as if going on a trip on a boat or airplane; discuss what you might need/want to take along (great for Dramatic Play Center)
- Provide each child with a paper airplane; allow them time to decorate; put masking tape starting line and have each child stand behind line and throw his airplane; see whose airplane flies farthest

Snack Idea:
- Stop Light Snack-break graham cracker into small sections; spread one small section with peanut butter and place a red, yellow and green M&M on to look like a stop light
- Eat Cheerios-pretend they are wheels
- Eat Spaghettios (for lunch today)-pretend they are wheels

Fieldtrip Ideas
- Visit car lot
- Visit local airport – pilots are usually willing to talk to the students and even let them look inside the plane

W

Color: Black

Number: 8

Shape: Octagon (stop sign)

Scripture: Go to the ant…consider her ways, and be wise. Proverbs 6:6

Theme: **Wiggly, Crawly Things**

Bible

- Scripture: Go to the ant…consider her ways, and be wise. Proverbs 6:6
- Tell the Story of the Ant. Keep it simple. The Bible says that we should be like the ant. An ant has no captain or ruler, but it knows to work hard storing food for the winter. We should be hard workers like the ant.
- Observe ants. Take a magnifying glass and carefully watch a few ants as they work. Put down a crumb and watch as they pick it up and carry it away. Place a large piece of bread down and come back later to see many ants at work.

Theme Learning

- Make a list on large chart paper of all the insects the children can name.
- Discuss how some wiggly and crawling creatures help us (bees make honey, worms are good for the soil, spiders catch bothersome flies, etc.)
- From Caterpillar to Butterfly – Read The Very Hungry Caterpillar by Eric Carle
- Discuss ants and how they work together; demonstrate by crumpling up sheets of paper (1 per child); put the crumpled paper in a laundry basket; spread in the center of the Circle and have only one child come up and pick them all up; note how long it took that one child to collect all those crumpled papers; now have all the children come up and pick up one piece and put it in the basket when you say go; note how fast the paper got picked up when we worked together

Letter Skills

- Say It: W says "w" like water
- Practice It: Get a plastic garden sprayer and fill with water; tell child if he can say "w" sound when asked what W says that you will mist the air with water and let him feel the rain
- Recognize It: Decorate Blank Letter W with "worms" (small pieces of yarn)
- Letter W box – fill empty wet wipes box with small items that begin with the letter W (water-in baby food jar, web-white yarn, toy watermelon slice, worm, etc.)
- W is for Worm – give each child a gummy worm (older preschoolers only) if he can say the correct sound "w" makes when asked
- W is for Watermelon – Cut out green oval from construction paper; cut out smaller pink oval and glue on top; this should resemble a watermelon that has been split in half; provide black stamp pad; if child can say the "w" sound correctly when asked, he may come up and press finger onto stamp pad and then press onto watermelon-making a fingerprint watermelon seed

Math
- Yard Stick Pick Up Bugs game-hot glue Velcro on end of yard stick or dowel rod; attach Velcro to small bug toys (party supply section usually has these); have child pick up bugs with ruler as he counts how many bugs he is catching
- Use Party Store insects for counting
- Purchase insect stickers (usually ladybug stickers are easy to find in card section); write the number 8 on paper and have child count and stick on 8 stickers
- Bumble Bee Number 8-let child shape black pipe cleaner to look like number 8 (wings); put wooden clothes pin in the middle (body of bee); to the clothes pin-glue on yellow and black small Pom Poms (alternate to look like stripes); this will make the cutest bumble bee; attach a magnet or hang from ceiling
- 8 Dots on a Ladybug game – Cut a red circle from felt; with Sharpie, draw lines for wings; cut 8 felt, black smaller circles; let children come up and put a dot on the ladybug as you count together; count backwards to remove; repeat (The felt should stick to each other without tape, much like a felt board)
- Spiders Have 8 Legs – show picture of a spider and count the legs together
  Sing: Spiders Have 8 Legs
  Spiders Have 8 Legs (tune of Mary Had a Little Lamb)
  Spi-ders have 8 Legs, 8 Legs, 8 Legs
  Spi-ders have 8 legs, 2 – 4 – 6 and 8
- Measure the Worm – measure Gummy Worms and record length (Note: you could take a picture of worm on table in advance and print out enough for each child to have one; they can glue picture to paper; write " ___ inches" at the bottom)

Shape Practice
- Sandpaper Rubbing-cut octagon shape from sandpaper, lay white paper on top and let child rub crayon over it, the sandpaper makes a neat texture crayon rubbing in the shape of the octagon; Note: works best if you peel the paper from crayon and color with crayon laying on it's side

- Stop Sign Bug game – instruct children to move like different insects that you call out, but when they see the stop sign go up, they should freeze (discuss the shape of the stop sign-octagon)

Color
- Wiggly Worm Tracks-run a piece of yarn through black paint and let child run the string along on white paper to make "worm tracks"
- Fingerprint Ants-use fingers dipped in black paint to make fingerprints all over white paper; add feet and antennae to these to look like little ants
- Spider Web-give child black construction paper; let him use white chalk to draw "spider webs"

Art
- Coffee Filter Butterfly- let child use markers to color coffee filter; when finished, have child spray the coffee filter with spray bottle filled with water; allow to dry; when dry, pinch in middle (wings) and clip with clothes pin (body); add wiggle eyes to clothes pin, and pipe cleaner antennae, if desired; hot glue magnet to back
- Egg Carton Caterpillar-cut cardboard egg carton in half so that child has six cups that are still connected and that look like a caterpillar; add wiggly eyes and pipe cleaner antennae
- Spider Hat-cut black construction paper in wide strip that will fit around child's head; cut out 8 small strips of black construction paper and fold "accordion" style back and forth…back and forth; glue these on for legs-four on each side; attach large wiggly eyes in front; child will LOVE wearing this spider hat
- Finger Print Spiders – use finger to make body and marker to draw on legs

Music
- Sing and act out, "The Ants Go Marching One By One…" Be sure to go all the way to number 8 (this week's number)
- Move Like A __ game - play music and move like the following: grasshopper, butterfly, worm, ant, spider, etc.
- Sing and act out the "Itsy Bitsy Spider" song
- Bumble Bee Dance-explain that bees dance to communicate; tell child to dance like he's happy, sad, excited, mad, etc.

Game Time
- Take a Walk-give children a magnifying glass; look for wiggly, crawly things; use shovel to dig up dirt and see if you uncover any earthworms; observe ants; etc.
- Mosquito Tag-purchase red colored small, round stickers from office supply section; invite friends over to play along; give "it" a page of red stickers and tell him if he catches anyone he is to put a red dot (mosquito bite) on him to show he's been tagged; try "biting" all players and then let someone else be the mosquito

Snack Idea

- Dirt and Worms-make chocolate pudding; crush chocolate sandwich cookies in Ziploc bag and sprinkle on pudding to look like dirt; add gummy worms (for older toddler)
- Ladybug Jigglers - let each child put 6 raisins in the bottom of a cupcake pan; have child pour Jello Jiggler liquid (pre-made) over raisins; when set, it will look like a ladybug (Note: premeasured liquid amount in small cup for child to pour into pan over his raisins; fill about 1/3 of the way; spray pan with cooking spray to help with release)

Fieldtrip Ideas

- Have a guest come in a talk about composting
- Have beekeeper come in and talk with the children
- Purchase live worms from a Bait Shop and read a book about worms
- Watch, "The Magic Schoolbus – In a Beehive"
- Watch, "A Bug's Life"

X

Color: Black
Number: 8
Shape: Octagon (stop sign)
Scripture: For we are His workmanship, created in Christ Jesus unto good works…
Ephesians 2:10

Theme: **X-Rays and Bones**

Bible

- Scripture: For we are His workmanship, created in Christ Jesus unto good works… Ephesians 2:10
- Tell the story of Samson. Keep it simple: God told Samson's parents that they would have a special baby. He would be super strong as long as they never cut his hair. When he grew up he continued to be strong. He even killed a lion with his bare hands. Samson led the people of Israel against the evil Philistine army. They wanted to capture Samson. After several tries, Samson's wife, Delilah, tricked him into telling her his secret. If his hair were to be cut, he wouldn't be strong anymore. The mean soldiers came and cut Samson's hair. Samson was blinded and had to work for the Philistines. A while later, Samson's hair grew back out. God helped him to be strong again and pull down the pillars that held up a great building where 5 Philistine king's were feasting.
- Grow Samson's Hair-decorate a Styrofoam cup with a face; put soil and grass seeds in the cup; in a matter of days the grass seeds will have sprouted and will need a hair cut

Theme Learning

- **What is an x-ray?** A photograph that uses a beam of high energy radiation that can pass through solid materials. This type photograph can be used to see organs inside the body and to determine if a bone is broken or a tooth has a cavity.

Our Bones

Without our bones, we would be floppy like a ragdoll. Our bones allow us to stand up straight, help us move, and protect our organs.

Bones are made up of three parts:
Compact bone – hard, outer layer
Spongy bone – softer, inner layer
Marrow-red marrow produces red and white blood cells; yellow marrow stores fat

Activity: Create a model of a bone by using an empty paper towel roll for the outer Compact Bone. Roll up rubber shelf liner and insert into the tube to represent the spongy bone. Finally stuff the tube with red and yellow pom poms to represent the marrow.

- **Our Skeleton**

  Our skeleton is made up of lots of different bones working together. When we are born, we have 300 bones. Some of the smaller bones grow together so that when we are adults we have 206 bones.

- **Movement**

  Tendons connect our bones to muscles which help us move.

  Protectors

  Some bones are very important since they protect our organs. Our skull acts like a helmet and protects our soft brain. Our spine protects the spinal cord which contains nerves that send messages from our brain telling the parts of our body how and when to move. Our ribs make a "cage" and protect our organs such as our heart, lungs, and liver.

- **Strong Bones**

  Strong bones need calcium. We should drink lots of milk and eat dairy products. Bones also need exercise.

Letter Skills
- Say It: X says "x" like xylophone
- Practice It: find old toy xylophone at flea market or Goodwill; if child can say "x" sound he may strike the xylophone
- Recognize It: Decorate Blank Letter X with colorful strips of construction paper like a toy xylophone
- Letter X box – fill empty wet wipes with items that begin with X (pictures of x-ray and xylophone, X-Men action figure, photo of Xavier Roberts-creator of Cabbage Patch Kids)
- X Bones – cut two white bone shapes from paper; glue onto another piece of construction paper to look like an X
- X says "ks" – the sound X makes is similar to the sound you hear when you use a spray bottle; simulate the sound; if child can correctly say "ks," give him a little mist with the squirt bottle
- XOXO – Hugs and Kisses game: hold up letter flashcards and instruct the children that when they see letter X, they should give themselves a big hug and blow a kiss (Explain that the letters XOXO stand for hugs and kisses.)

Math
- French Fry Counting-purchase inexpensive yellow sponges and cut them in strips to resemble French fries; use small white envelopes for the fry holders; write numbers on each envelope and draw dots beside each number to make it easier; have child count the dots and put that number of fries into correct holder
- Popsicle Stick Bone counting-pretend Popsicle sticks are bones and try to count to number 8 (Use for Circle Time…count one at a time)

- Dig Up 8 Skeletons – Add party favor skeletons (you can purchase these around Halloween) in the Sand Table…if you don't have a sand table, make a simple one using a plastic storage container filled with sand; bury the skeletons and let children use tongs to pick up; tell them they should count 8 skeletons
- Bone Patterns – cut bone shapes from various colors of construction paper; arrange in a pattern and have children tell you what comes next; repeat with different patterns (Ex. 2 blue – 2 red – 2 blue – 2 red…)
- Elevator Counting – cut a piece of construction paper in half lengthwise; cut out 8 circles and glue to construction paper to resemble elevator buttons; instruct each child to come up and push the number you call out (Explain that x-rays are taken at a hospital…hospitals usually have elevators)

Shape Practice
- Octagon Cutting-octagons are easy to cut since it is made up of straight lines; give your child safety scissors and let him cut along a pre-drawn line
- Shaving Crème Number Practice-squirt white shaving crème on table and spread out; let child practice drawing octagons
- Traffic Sign Patterns – cut out the traffic signs (on the next page); arrange in a pattern and have children tell you what should come next (Remind the children that the stop sign shape is called an octagon)
- Feel the Shape – cut shapes from cardboard cereal box; place in a sack and let children take turns reaching in and guessing what shape they feel; they must think…how many sides do I feel…how many points, etc.

Color
- Make an X-Ray drawing-trace child's hand on black paper using white crayon; let him draw lines to show the bones in hand using the same white chalk
- Look at a real X-Ray-borrow an old x-ray from a chiropractor's office (they usually have old ones that they would be willing to give you); discuss black background versus white bone images
- X-ray Glasses – put on plastic toy glasses and have children look around for the color black around the room (you can purchase a pack of party favor sunglasses to use or check with your local movie theater to see if they will donate enough pairs of 3D Glasses…you can pop out the lenses) Explain that in fictional books and movies, the hero sometimes has x-ray glasses which can see through walls.)

Art
- Q-tip Skeleton – glue head and Q-tips for form skeleton (see photos and template on next page); you may pre-draw lines showing children where to glue the bones
- X-ray Painting-dip child's hand in white paint and press on black paper to look like x-ray (Can use child's own picture cut in circle shape for head…these would be cute on a bulletin board)
- Greeting Card Collage – Explain that when you are sick and need to go the hospital for x-rays, sometimes people will send Get Well Cards; cut around the colorful pictures on the front of old Greeting Cards and let children each make a

collage (ask parents to help collect old cards…stores that sell cards often will donate the old ones they need to rotate)

- Milk Jug Skeleton – must have parents save milk jugs for a long time in advance or check with local recycling center; freehand various bones as shown – there are 8 arm & leg bones; trace children's own hands and feet; this is a detailed project, so you may want to just make one for display in the class (see following pages for mouth template)

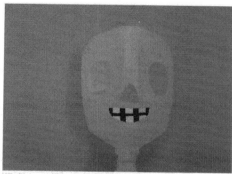

Skeleton with paper mouth

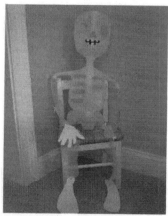

Skeleton with paper hands and feet-the students each traced and cut out their own hands and feet

Music
- Play toy xylophone
- Bone Pokey-put your arm bone in, put your leg bone in, put your skull in, etc.
- X-ray – played like "Freeze;" play lively music and let children dance around; when the music stops, they must say x-ray and freeze (Explain that you have to hold very still when an x-ray is being taken)

Game Time
- Play "Doggy, Doggy, Where's Your Bone" but use "Skeleton, Skeleton, Where's Your Bone;" use stuffed white tube sock for bone; let child try to find where you hid bone
- Xerox Game – explain that Xerox starts with x and is used to make copies; tell the children that we will copy what the leader does

Snack Idea
- Pretzel Stick "bones"
- Marshmallow Skeleton-use large marshmallow for head and smaller marshmallows for other bones; affix with white frosting
- Biscuit Bones-pinch in middle of canned biscuit to form bone shape; bake and eat bones

Fieldtrip Ideas
- Take "fieldtrip" to local orthopedist to see replica of human skeleton
- Watch, "The Magic School Bus – Inside the Human Body"

Y
Color: Purple
Number: 9
Shape: Oval
Scripture: And God made two great lights; the greater light to rule the day, and the lesser light to rule the night: he made the stars also. Genesis 1:16

Theme: **Yippee, Summer Is Here!**

Bible
- Scripture: <u>And God made two great lights</u>; the greater light to rule the day, and the lesser light to rule the night: he made the stars also. Genesis 1:16 (young preschoolers could just learn the underlined part above)
- Tell the Creation Story. Keep it simple. Go over the Days of Creation using the list below. Spend time discussing the sun/moon.
  - Day 1- Day & Night
  - Day 2- Sky
  - Day 3- Land & Sea
  - Day 4- Sun, Moon, & Stars
  - Day 5- Fish & Birds
  - Day 6- Animals and Man
  - Day 7- God rested

Theme Learning
- Disc. seasons – name all 4 seasons and discuss the differences
  Spring – flowers bud, weather gets warmer
  Summer – grass needs to be mowed, very hot outside, wear shorts
  Fall – cooler weather, leaves changes and fall, wear jacket & long pants
  Winter – cold outside, leaves sometimes snows, wear coats and boots
- Discuss the activities people do during summer time: picnics, ride bikes, 4th of July Fireworks, camping, fishing, take vacations, etc.
- Discuss summer vacations – discuss where people usually go on vacation: beach, mountains, Disney World/Land, etc. (show travel brochures you can pick up from a local travel agency or Chamber of Commerce); make a list of trips the kids can remember taking
- Discuss the temperature – explain that we use a thermometer to let us know how hot or cold it is outside; in ummer, the red mercury inside rises; in Winter, it goes way down; sometimes is can even get 100 degrees during Summer

Letter Skills
- Say It: Y says "y" like yarn
- Practice It: Yarn Catch-toss ball of yarn to child and have him say "y" sound; when he tosses it back to you, say "y" sound; continue several times
- Recognize It: Decorate Blank letter Y by gluing on pieces of yarn
- Letter Y box – fill empty wet wipes container with small items that begin with letter Y (yarn, yellow crayon, yo-yo, etc.)

- Y is for Yellow Like the Sun painting – fingerpaint a letter Y cutout
- Yell for Letter Y – show flashcards and instruct the students that when they see letter Y, they should yell; have both upper and lower case Y's included and continue to stick them back in the deck
- Y is for Yam – cut a yam in half; put some paint in paper plates; let the children use the yam to stamp white construction paper; write heading Y is for Yam on the paper

Math

- Sunflower Seed Counting-have child count and glue 9 sunflower seeds to black dessert sized, paper plate; add yellow construction paper petals to make a sunflower
- Beach Ball Numbers-write numbers 1-9 on beach ball; roll ball to child and have him say number that is on top of ball when it lands; continue until all the numbers have been read
- Sandpaper Sandcastle – cut simple castle shape from sandpaper; have child glue to blue construction paper; add 9 sea shell stickers
- Sea Shell Counting – have children help you count sea shells aloud 1-9
- Beach Ball Counting – toss a colorful beach ball high in the air and have children count the number of tosses 1-9

Shape Practice

- Paint the sidewalk-give child bucket of water and large paintbrush; have him paint ovals on the sidewalk with water and watch as the sun dries the water and makes them disappear
- Sun Print Oval-cut out oval shape from cereal box cardboard; take black piece of construction paper outside on a sunny summer day and have child put oval on top of black paper (may need to secure with tape on back of oval so that it doesn't blow away); go back later and you'll find that the sun has faded the black paper; lift up the cardboard oval to reveal a dark black oval shape (Note: do this on Monday and check on Friday to see the oval print)
- Yam – show a yam and discuss how it looks oval
- Pass the Oval – hard boil an egg and peel; let children pass it around and feel the shape of an oval; when finished, break it open and show the yolk (Remind them that letter y says "y" like yolk.)

Color

- Golf Ball Painting-dip golf ball in purple paint; put white paper inside old box and let child put golf ball on top of paper in box and roll around to make purple stripes on paper
- Colorful Sand-color water with purple food coloring; pour colored water into garden spray bottle; let child spray the sand purple, when it dries it will be a beautiful, colorful oasis (messy, but fun)
- Seeing Purple – look around for things that are purple in the room; make a list of other things that are purple (grapes, purple crayon, etc.)

Art

- Watermelon-cut watermelon shape and have child use fingerprints to paint on black seeds
- Special Summer Time Shower Curtain Display-purchase inexpensive blue shower curtain and cheap pair of flip flops from dollar type store; pour paint into paper plate and let child step in paint while wearing the flip flops and walk across shower curtain; use permanent marker to write, "We've flipped For Summer!"; when footprints are dry don't forget to go back with paint to add lines for the part on top of flip flops that hold feet in; paint on a bright yellow sun and beach scene if you'd like
- Sun Catcher-cut two identical circular shapes from contact paper; peel one side off and let child attach pieces of colorful tissue paper squares; put other piece on top and hang with yarn in window as a sun catcher
- Sea Shell Frame-have each child glue sea shells to inexpensive wooden frame (or cut frame shape from cereal box cardboard and attach magnet); add child's photo
- Summer Snow Globe – Spray paint lids of clean baby food jars in advance; let children fill with water and add tiny drop of food coloring, glitter and a small sea shell; tighten lid and secure with hot glue

Music

- Sing, "You Are My Sunshine;" make simple hand puppets by stapling two dessert sized, yellow plates all the way around except for the
- Ice Cream Carton Drum-wash empty ice cream containers and use for drums
- Soda Shaker-fill empty 2 Liter soda bottle with dry beans and shake away to the beat of favorite music CD or radio
- Freeze Game-when it's hot outside, play "freeze" inside; play lively music and tell child when the music stops he is to "freeze"

Game Time

- Homemade Slip and Slide-get large tarp and spread across backyard; squirt bottle of tear-free baby shampoo all over tarp; use water hose to wet tarp and slide away (careful, very slippery)
- Sprinkler time-put bathing suits on and go out and have fun under the sprinkle; bring out beach towels and don't forget to open up the sandbox
- Super Cool Kiddie Pool-fill kid size pool with water and add a bag of ice you purchase or empty ice from your ice maker into pool; the ice really makes a fun and very "cool" addition
- Bubbles-give your children store bought or homemade bubbles (dish detergent and water) and let them blow bubbles; try using other items for bubble wand such as fly swatter for tons of tiny bubbles, straw (for older child), empty toilet roll, etc.
- Freeze Tag – fill spray bottle with ice water; have children move around and when you mist them they must "freeze" in place; the last child standing wins the game (This game would make a great outdoor game.)

Snack Idea
- Enjoy Popsicles outside or make homemade Popsicles using Kool Aid, clean yogurt cups, and craft sticks
- Ocean and Sand Snack-make blue Jell-O and let set; crush graham crackers in zip lock and sprinkle around outer edges to resemble "sand"

Fieldtrip Ideas
- Have a Water Fun Day – send a note home asking that children wear swimsuits under clothes and a change of clothes and towel; see Game Time for several ideas

Z
Color: Purple
Number: 10
Shape: Oval
Scripture: For the Son of Man is come to seek and to save that which was lost.
Luke 19:10

Theme: **Zoo**

Bible
- Scripture: For the Son of Man is come to seek and to save that which was lost. Luke 19:10
- Tell story of Zachaeus
- Make Sycamore Tree-paint child's hand (branches) and top of arm (trunk) brown; press onto white paper; add green fingerprint leaves
- Sing "Zachaeus Was a Wee Little Man"

Theme Learning
- What is a zoo? A zoo is a place for animals to live; scientists study the animals at a zoo to learn more about them; people come to see the animals in the zoo
- What kinds of animals live in the zoo? zebras, girraffs, hippos, monkeys, kangaroo, snakes, birds, etc
- Zoo animals needs – food, water, shelter
- Zoo Keeper/Veterinarian – A zoo keeper takes care of the animals and makes sure their needs are met; a veterinarian is an animal doctor that takes care of animals that are sick

Letter Skills
- Say It-Z says "z" like zipper
- Practice It-cut zippers from old jeans or purchase inexpensive, used pants from Goodwill; let child practice zipping the zippers as he says "z" sound
- Recognize It: Decorate Blank Letter Z with zebra stripes made by making lines across Z with black paint and Q-tip (or black crayon)
- Letter Z box – add small items that begin with Z to an empty wet wipes container (zipper, zero, toy zebra, zinnia, etc.)
- Z is for Zucchini – cut a zucchini in half and use for stamping; write heading Z is for Zucchini; use several and let children make lots of colorful zucchini circular prints

Math
- Animal Cracker Counters-use animal crackers to count 10 zoo animals
- Teddy Grahams Counters – write numbers 1 – 10 on paper cups; let child count out and add teddy grahams equaling the numbers listed in the cups
- Animal Sorting-have children sort stuffed animals according to kind, color, size, etc.

- Zoo Animal Counters-purchase small bag of plastic zoo animals from party store and let child count them
- Barrel of Monkey Counting – have children come up and link another monkey as you count together 1 – 10
- Zoo Animal Patterns – put various animal stickers on index cards; show the children a pattern and see if they can tell you what comes next (giraffe-giraff-monkey…giraffe-giraffe, __); repeat with different animals and patterns
- Feed the Animals Toss – give children bean bags and pail and allow them to try to feed the animals by ringing the bucket with the bean bag

Shape Practice
- Toothpaste Ovals-buy inexpensive toothpaste from dollar type store and let child use it as he would a marker by having him squeeze the tube and form ovals on wax paper; child will retain learning much better as oppose to using ordinary marker
- Oval Eggs-some birds like flamingos live at the zoo; cut out oval egg shapes; glue Easter grass to blue construction paper and then glue the eggs in the grass
- Oval Bear – Demonstrate for children how to draw a bear using only ovals as shown; older preschoolers may wish to try to draw one too

Color
- Make Purple-have child stir blue and red paint together to make purple
- Make "Purple Cows" by pouring purple soda over vanilla ice cream
- Purple Jelly-let child spread breakfast toast with purple jelly to reinforce this week's color
- Show red and blue make purple – fill clear class with water; add a few drops of blue paint; add a few drops of red paint; stir with straw and watch the water turn purple

Art
- Caged Zoo Animals-cut animal pictures from magazines; glue to back of inside of a shoe box; punch holes on top and bottom of shoe box aligned all the way down; stick straws into holes to resemble bars of cage

- Caged Zoo Animals (another version) – use Styrofoam meat tray instead of box; glue animals, grass, and tree; poke holes and thread black thread through the holes to resemble bars; secure with tape at the back
- Giraffe w/ Spots that Stands - cut giraffe shape from yellow construction paper and mount on cereal box cardboard; use brown paint and Q-tip to paint on brown spots; attach two clothes pins for legs and he will really stand up
- Zebra Stripes-Google for horse coloring sheet; dip golf ball in black paint and have child roll ball around on top of horse picture to make zebra stripes (works best with coloring sheet in shallow copy paper box top)
- Zoo Animal Play Dough – roll play dough in the shape of a snake and bend around to form letter Z

Music
- Tap Dancing-attach baby food jar lids securely to bottom of child's shoes using rubber bands; play music and let them tap dance on hard floor
- PVC pipe flute-cut small section from PVC pipe; drill holes in pipe and let child play it like a flute
- Sing and act out, "Five Little Monkeys Jumping on the Bed"
- Sing "The Animal in the Zoo" as you would "The Wheels on the Bus" by using bears in the zoo…growl, kangaroos…hop, elephants…trumpet sound, etc.

Game Time
- Zoo Movement Game-move like an elephant, zebra, snake, flamingo, bear, etc.
- Penguin Race-have child place balloon between legs and waddle like penguin; try having a penguin race
- Zoo Keeper May I? game - played like Mother May I
- Monkey, Monkey, Bear game – played like Duck, Duck, Goose
- Pass the Grumpy Bear – played like Hot Potato; tell kids the bear is grumpy and you don't want to hold him too long; when the music stops, whoever has the bear must roar like a grumpy bear

Snack Idea
- Keebler Zebra Striped cookies
- Little Debbie-Zebra Cakes (actually have picture of zebra on box)
- Animal Crackers
- Graham Cracker Zoo-spread white icing on graham cracker; put animal crackers on top of icing; put black licorice stripes on top of everything to create zoo cage
- Banana Split variation – let children use plastic butter knife to cut ripe banana into slices; add whipped cream and some chocolate syrup   (tell children that monkeys love bananas)

Fieldtrip Ideas
- Visit a zoo, if you have one close by
- Have a last day of school party with zoo themed plates, napkins, etc. The theme could be, "Have a Wild Summer!"

Weekly Lesson Plan Theme: Apples

Small Group Time:
1.Letter Skills
2.Numbers/Readiness Skills
3-Art or Cooking

Story Time left blank so you can fill in with titles your library has...try to find books related to the theme

	Monday	Tuesday	Wednesday	Thursday	Friday
Bible Time	Read Bible verse Tell Story of Adam and Eve	Review Bible verse Prayer Time (use small white board to record/erase requests and praises)	Review Bible verse Prayer Time	Review Bible verse Prayer Time	Review Bible story Review Bible verse Prayer Time
Greeting Circle	Star Student Read Care Bear Journal Calendar/Weather Routine Birthdays & Share Bears (4)	Good Morning song Calendar/Weather Routine Birthdays Share Bears (4)	Good Morning song Calendar/Weather Routine Birthdays Share Bears (4)	Good Morning song Calendar/Weather Routine Birthdays Share Bears (4)	Good Morning song Calendar/Weather Routine Birthdays Share Bears (4)
Center Time/ Small Group Time	1. Blank A/fingerprint ants 2. Apple Seed Sheet (math) 3.Apple Stamping	1-A-a-a choo Tissue sheet 2-String Apple Jacks (math) 3. Stained Glass Apples	1.Look through A box 2.Sort apples (color) 3.Handprint apple tree	1.no letter activity for today 2.Add stickers to tree (shape) 3.Cooking-applesauce	F I E
Circle Time	Theme-How Apples Grow Letter Skills-Intro. Letter A Math Skills-cut apple,count seeds Color/Shape-discuss red & circle	Theme- Apple Colors Letter Skills-"a-a-a-choo" game Math Skills-show how to write 1 Color/Shape-pass aro. toilet paper binoculars...look for red & circles	Theme-Apple Seeds Letter Skills-Letter A box Math Skills-sky write 1 Color/Shape-pass out magazines, look for red...glue to large poster board to make class collage	Theme-Plant Apple Seed Letter Skills-Review Math Skills-Review Color-review red Shape-review circle	L D T
Story Time	Read book:	Read book:	Read book:	Read book:	R I P
Game Time/Music	Pickin' Apples game	Batter Up game	Apples Fallin' Down	Ant, Ant, Anteater (played like Duck, Duck, Goose) or Follow the Leader like ants do	Suggestions: apple orchard or grocery store-produce section
Closing Circle	Review today's theme, letter and math skills, color and shape	Review today's theme, letter and math skills, color and shape	Review today's theme, letter and math skills, color and shape	Review today's theme, letter and math skills, color and shape	Review this week's theme, letter, math, color, shape Pass out Care Bear backpack & Star Student briefcase

Weekly Lesson Plan — Theme: Bears and Camping

Letter: B
Color: red
Number: 1
Shape: circle
Scripture: Hebrews 13:6

Small Group Time:
1. Letter Skills
2. Numbers/Readiness Skills
3- Art or Cooking

	Monday	Tuesday	Wednesday	Thursday	Friday
Bible Time	Read Bible verse. Tell Story of David and Goliath	Review Bible verse. Prayer Time (use small white board to record/erase requests and praises)	Review Bible verse. Prayer Time	Review Bible verse. Prayer Time	Review Bible story. Review Bible verse. Prayer Time
Greeting Circle	Star Student. Read Care Bear Journal. Calendar/Weather Routine. Birthdays & Share Bears (4)	Good Morning song. Calendar/Weather Routine. Birthdays. Share Bears (4)	Good Morning song. Calendar/Weather Routine. Birthdays. Share Bears (4)	Good Morning song. Calendar/Weather Routine. Birthdays. Share Bears (4)	Good Morning song. Calendar/Weather Routine. Birthdays. Share Bears (4)
Center/ Small Group Time	1. Decorate blank letter B with bandaids. 2. Practice writing number 1 in sandbox. 3. Paint red "campfire"	1. Use beans as manipulatives to write B. 2. Make bean shaker (music). 3. Bubble painting	1. Look through Letter B box. 2. Go Fishing game. 3. Decorate brown bags to put trail mix in (tomorrow)	1. Letter B collage from magazines. 2. no math activity for today. 3. Cooking-Make trail mix	F I E L D T R I P
Circle Time	Theme-Discuss what you might need to take when camping? Letter Skills-Intro. Letter B. Math Skills-sky write number 1. Color/Shape-discuss red & circle	Theme-Where might you camp? Show brochures. Letter Skills-"b" like bubles game. Math Skills-count the bubbles. Color/Shape-pass aro. toilet paper binoculars...look for red & circles	Theme-What might you do on your camping trip? Letter Skills-Letter B box. Math Skills-Go Fishing game/count magazines, look for red...glue to large poster	Theme-What kinds of wildlife might you see. Letter Skills-Review. Math Skills-Review. Color/Shape-show how to make circle bear (will be making for Art)	
Story Time	Read book:	Read book:	Read book:	Read book:	
Game Time/Music	Game: Bean bag toss	Music: Bean shakers/music	Game: While music plays Pass the ball (when the music stops, must tell something that starts with B)	Music: Going on a Bear Hunt song and Teddy Bear, Teddy Bear Turn Around song	Suggestions: "Camping Trip" outside. Smokey Bear visit. Local state park
Closing Circle	Review today's theme, letter and math skills, color and shape	Review today's theme, letter and math skills, color and shape	Review today's theme, letter and math skills, color and shape	Review today's theme, letter and math skills, color and shape	Review this week's theme, letter, math, color, shape. Pass out Care Bear backpack & Star Student briefcase

Weekly Lesson Plan   Theme: Circus Carnival/Clowns

Letter: C   Number: 1
Color: red   Shape: circle
Scripture: Prov. 16:20

Small Group Time:
1. Letter Skills
2. Numbers/Readiness Skills
3- Art or Cooking

	Monday	Tuesday	Wednesday	Thursday	Friday
Bible Time	Read Bible verse Tell Story of Daniel in the Lion Den	Review Bible verse Prayer Time (use small white board to record/erase requests and praises)	Review Bible verse Prayer Time	Review Bible verse Prayer Time	Review Bible story Review Bible verse Prayer Time
Greeting Circle	Star Student Read Care Bear Journal Class Jobs Calendar/Weather Routine Birthdays & Share Bears (4)	Good Morning song Calendar/Weather Routine Birthdays Share Bears (4)	Good Morning song Calendar/Weather Routine Birthdays Share Bears (4)	Good Morning song Calendar/Weather Routine Birthdays Share Bears (4)	Good Morning song Calendar/Weather Routine Birthdays Share Bears (4)
Center Time/ Small Group Time	1. Decorate blank letter C with cotton balls 2. Shaving creme-write 1 3. Make paper plate lion (from Bible time)	1. Shape pipe cleaner like C 2. Circus Animal cracker counters 3. Circle stamping-use toilet roll end or potato	1. Look through Letter C box 2. Draw circus tent and glue animal crackers 3. Handprint elephant	1. Letter C collage from magazines 2. no math activity for today 3. Cooking-Make homemade crayons	F I E
Circle Time	Theme-What might you see at a circus? Letter Skills-Intro. Letter B Math Skills-sky write number 1 Color/Shape-discuss red & circle	Theme-What animals you might see at a circus? Letter Skills-"c" like clown game Math Skills-count the clown spots Color/Shape-put a red circle on each child's nose using face paint	Theme-What things might be happening at a circus? Letter Skills-Letter C box Math Skills-Go Fishing game/count Color/Shape-play "I Spy" red things	Theme-What does it take to be ready for the circus? Letter Skills-Review Math Skills-Review Color/Shape-Review	L D T
Story Time	Read book:	Read book:	Read book:	Read book:	R I P
Game Time/Music	Game: Balloon Toss game	Music: Move like Circus Animals	Game: Tightrope Walking	Game: Jumping Through Hoops	Suggestions: Show the movie, "Dumbo" Have a balloon artist or clown visit the class
Closing Circle	Review today's theme, letter and math skills, color and shape	Review today's theme, letter and math skills, color and shape	Review today's theme, letter and math skills, color and shape	Review today's theme, letter and math skills, color and shape	Review this week's theme, letter, math, color, shape Pass out Care Bear backpack & Star Student briefcase

Weekly Lesson Plan — Theme: Down on the Farm

Letter: D. Number: 1 Scripture:
Color: red Shape: circle Eccl. 3:1-2

Small Group Time:
1. Letter Skills
2. Numbers/Readiness Skills
3-Art or Cooking

	Monday	Tuesday	Wednesday	Thursday	Friday
Bible Time	Read Bible verse Tell Story of The Sower	Review Bible verse Prayer Time (use small white board to record/erase requests and praises)	Review Bible verse Prayer Time	Review Bible verse Prayer Time	Review Bible story Review Bible verse Prayer Time
Greeting Circle	Star Student Read Care Bear Journal Class Jobs Calendar/Weather Routine Birthdays & Share Bears (4)	Good Morning song Calendar/Weather Routine Birthdays Share Bears (4)	Good Morning song Calendar/Weather Routine Birthdays Share Bears (4)	Good Morning song Calendar/Weather Routine Birthdays Share Bears (4)	Good Morning song Calendar/Weather Routine Birthdays Share Bears (4)
Center Time/ Small Group Time	1. Decorate blank letter D with dalmation dots 2. Dog Bone Activity 3. Pig nose (see Art)	1. Feed the Pigs activitiy 2. Mud painting-lots of 1's 3. Sticker Farm Scene (see Art)	1. Playdough-form F, f 2. Haystack counting 3. Tractor tracks painting (see Art)	1. Letter F hunt 2. Circle Mobile (shape) 3. Cooking-homemade butter	F I E
Circle Time	Theme-What might you find on a farm? Letter Skills-Intro. Letter D Math Skills-sky write number 1 Color/Shape-discuss red & circle	Theme-Discuss gardens Letter Skills-"c" like clown game Math Skills-count the clown spots Color/Shape-put a red circle on each child's nose using face paint	Theme-Discuss the work the farmer does Letter Skills-Letter C box Math Skills-Go Fishing game/count Color/Shape-play "I Spy" red things	Theme-Discuss animals on the farm Letter Skills-Review Math Skills-Review Color/Shape-Review	L D T R I P
Story Time	Read book:	Read book:	Read book:	Read book:	
Game Time/Music	Game: Doggy, Doggy, Where's Your Bone game	Game: Pin the Tale on the Piggy	Game: Milk the Cow	Game: Sing "Old McDonald" and "Where Oh Where..." and "The Animals on the Farm Go..."	Suggestions: visit a local farm or petting zoo visit a Farmer's Market
Closing Circle	Review today's theme, letter and math skills, color and shape	Review today's theme, letter and math skills, color and shape	Review today's theme, letter and math skills, color and shape	Review today's theme, letter and math skills, color and shape	Review this week's theme, letter, math, color, shape Pass out Care Bear backpack & Star Student briefcase

Weekly Lesson Plan   Theme: Emotions/Feelings

	Letter: E	Number: 2	Scripture:
	Color: orange	Shape: square	James 1:5

Small Group Time:
1.Letter Skills
2.Numbers/Readiness Skills
3-Art or Cooking

	Monday	Tuesday	Wednesday	Thursday	Friday
Bible Time	Read Bible verse Tell Story of Soloman	Review Bible verse Prayer Time (use small white board to record/erase requests and praises)	Review Bible verse Prayer Time	Review Bible verse Prayer Time	Review Bible story Review Bible verse Prayer Time
Greeting Circle	Star Student Read Care Bear Journal Class Jobs Calendar/Weather Routine Birthdays & Share Bears (4)	Good Morning song Calendar/Weather Routine Birthdays Share Bears (4)	Good Morning song Calendar/Weather Routine Birthdays Share Bears (4)	Good Morning song Calendar/Weather Routine Birthdays Share Bears (4)	Good Morning song Calendar/Weather Routine Birthdays Share Bears (4)
Center Time/ Small Group Time	1. Decorate blank letter E with egg shells 2. Trace number 2 3. Feelings collage	1. 2.Numbers 1 and 2 rubbings with pennies 3.Watercolor paint with feeling (see Art)	1. 2.Count pairs of objects 3.Paper plate happy face	1.Letter Hunt-E 2.Squares collage (see Shapes) 3.Cooking-rice cake smiley face	F I E L D T R I P
Circle Time	Theme-What are emotions? Letter Skills-Intro. Letter E Math Skills-Intro. number 2 Color/Shape-Intro. orange, square	Theme-What might cause our emotions? Letter Skills-E says "eh" like little old lady activity Math Skills- Color/Shape-	Theme-Recognize others emotions (magazine pictures) Letter Skills- Letter E box Math Skills- Color/Shape-I Spy Squares game	Theme-Disc. properly showing emotions Letter Skills-Review Math Skills-Review Color/Shape-Review	
Story Time	Read book:	Read book:	Read book:	Read book:	
Game Time/Music	Game: Happy/Sad Sorting	Music: "If You're Happy and You Know It" song	Game: Bean bag game	Music: Music with stomping, jumping, etc. (see Music)	Suggestions: Brewsters or other ice cream shop
Closing Circle	Review today's theme, letter and math skills, color and shape	Review today's theme, letter and math skills, color and shape	Review today's theme, letter and math skills, color and shape	Review today's theme, letter and math skills, color and shape	Review this week's theme, letter, math, color, shape Pass out Care Bear backpack & Star Student briefcase

Weekly Lesson Plan   Theme: Fish

Letter: F   Number: 2   Scripture:
Color: orange   Shape: square   Luke 11:28

Small Group Time:
1. Letter Skills
2. Numbers/Readiness Skills
3- Art or Cooking

	Monday	Tuesday	Wednesday	Thursday	Friday
Bible Time	Read Bible verse. Tell Story of Jonah and the Big Fish	Review Bible verse. Prayer Time (use small white board to record/erase requests and praises)	Review Bible verse. Prayer Time	Review Bible verse. Prayer Time	Review Bible story. Review Bible verse. Prayer Time
Greeting Circle	Star Student. Read Care Bear Journal. Class Jobs. Calendar/Weather Routine. Birthdays & Share Bears (4)	Good Morning song. Calendar/Weather Routine. Birthdays. Share Bears (4)	Good Morning song. Calendar/Weather Routine. Birthdays. Share Bears (4)	Good Morning song. Calendar/Weather Routine. Birthdays. Share Bears (4)	Good Morning song. Calendar/Weather Routine. Birthdays. Share Bears (4)
Center Time/ Small Group Time	1. Decorate blank F with fingerprints 2. 2 Fish in Ziplock fish bowl craft (see Numbers) 3. Brown Bag Big Fish (Bible)	1. Fishing Game (Letters) 2. Shape practice-square play area (see Shapes) 3. Paint an orange goldfish	1. Letter F Hunt 2. Seashell impressions (see Color) 3. Fish Bowl Craft	1. F collage 2. no activity today 3. Cooking-Peanut butter and pretzel fishing or blue jello with gummyfish	F; I; E
Circle Time	Theme- Where do fish live? Letter Skills-Intro. letter F. Math Skills-Disc. number 2. Color/Shape-Disc. orange, square	Theme- What kinds of fish live in ponds, lakes and rivers? Letter Skills- F says "f" like fish. Math Skills- Beach towel counting. Color/Shape-Square play area (see Shapes)	Theme- What kinds of fish live in the oceans? Letter Skills- Letter F box. Math Skills- Fishing pole/counting. Color/Shape-"I Spy" orange squares	Theme- What kind of fish are pets and what are their needs? Letter Skills-Review. Math Skills-Review. Color/Shape-Review	L; D; T
Story Time	Read book:	Read book:	Read book:	Read book:	R; I; P
Game Time/Music	Music-Fish Hokey Pokey	Game-Fly Swatter Bubbles	Game-Dive Under the Ocean	Game-Fish, Fish, Shark (like Duck, Duck, Goose)	Suggestions: Aquarium. Watch Nemo
Closing Circle	Review today's theme, letter and math skills, color and shape	Review today's theme, letter and math skills, color and shape	Review today's theme, letter and math skills, color and shape	Review today's theme, letter and math skills, color and shape	Review this week's theme, letter, math, color, shape. Pass out Care Bear backpack & Star Student briefcase

Weekly Lesson Plan   Theme: Mother Goose Rhymes

	Letter: G	Number: 2	Scripture:
	Color: orange	Shape: square	1 Peter 5:7

Small GroupTime:
1.Letter Skills
2.Numbers/Readiness Skills
3-Art or Cooking

	Monday	Tuesday	Wednesday	Thursday	Friday
Bible Time	Read Bible verse Tell Story of The Lost Sheep	Review Bible verse Prayer Time (use small white board to record/erase requests and praises)	Review Bible verse Prayer Time	Review Bible verse Prayer Time	Review Bible story Review Bible verse Prayer Time
Greeting Circle	Star Student Read Care Bear Journal Class Jobs Calendar/Weather Routine Birthdays & Share Bears (4)	Good Morning song Calendar/Weather Routine Birthdays Share Bears (4)	Good Morning song Calendar/Weather Routine Birthdays Share Bears (4)	Good Morning song Calendar/Weather Routine Birthdays Share Bears (4)	Good Morning song Calendar/Weather Routine Birthdays Share Bears (4)
Center Time/ Small Group Time	1. Decorate blank G with glitter 2. Mitten Lacing 3. Toilet roll Candlestick	1.Playdough G's 2. Egg Carton Counting 3. Handprint Sheep	1.Letter G Hunt 2. Egg Mosaid (see Color) 3.Old Woman Who Lived in Shoe collage	1.no activity today 2.Make Orange (see Color) 3.Cooking: Make Muffin Man Muffins	F I E L D T R I P
Circle Time	Theme-Who was Mother Goose? Letter Skills-Intro. letter G Math Skills-Disc. number 2 Color/Shape-Disc. orange, square	Theme-Humpty Dumpty Letter Skills-g says "g" like gum Math Skills- Roll the dice Color/Shape-Square Wall (see Shapes)	Theme-Little Bo Peep Letter Skills- Feed the Monster Math Skills- graph fav. nursery rhyme Color/Shape-	Theme-Name that rhyme game Letter Skills-Review Math Skills-Review Color/Shape-Review	
Story Time	Read book:	Read book:	Read book:	Read book:	
Game Time/Music	Game-Jack be Nimble	Game-Shepherd, Shepherd, Where's Your Sheep?	Music-Hey Diddle Diddle	Music-Twinkle, Twinkle Little Star	Suggestions: Library Show movie, "Barney-Mother Goose"
Closing Circle	Review today's theme, letter and math skills, color and shape	Review today's theme, letter and math skills, color and shape	Review today's theme, letter and math skills, color and shape	Review today's theme, letter and math skills, color and shape	Review this week's theme, letter, math, color, shape Pass out Care Bear backpack & Star Student briefcase

Weekly Lesson Plan

Theme: Special Holiday:
Fall Festival/Halloween (Christian Version)

	Letter: review	Number: 2	Scripture:
	Color: orange	Shape: square	Ps. 51:10

Small GroupTime:
1. Letter Skills
2. Numbers/Readiness Skills
3-Art or Cooking

	Monday	Tuesday	Wednesday	Thursday	Friday
Bible Time	Read Bible verse Tell Story of the Christian Pumpkin	Review Bible verse Prayer Time (use small white board to record/erase requests and praises)	Review Bible verse Prayer Time	Review Bible verse Prayer Time	Review Bible story Review Bible verse Prayer Time
Greeting Circle	Star Student Read Care Bear Journal Class Jobs Calendar/Weather Routine Birthdays & Share Bears (4)	Good Morning song Calendar/Weather Routine Birthdays Share Bears (4)	Good Morning song Calendar/Weather Routine Birthdays Share Bears (4)	Good Morning song Calendar/Weather Routine Birthdays Share Bears (4)	Good Morning song Calendar/Weather Routine Birthdays Share Bears (4)
Center Time/ Small Group Time	1. Trace alphabet magnets 2. Orange stamping (see Color) 3. Fall Festival Treat Bucket	1. Alphabet stamping 2. Orange play dough (see Color) 3. Decorate mini pumpkins	1. Playdough with alphabet cookie cutters 2. Fingerpaint with orange (see Color) 3. Add yarn and seeds	1. no activity today 2. Sort the Squares (see Shape) 3. Cooking: Pumpkin Tortillas	F I E
Circle Time	Theme- Read From Seed to Pumpkin by: Wendy Pfefier Letter Skills-What's the Sound song Math Skills-Count orange seeds (see below) Color/Shape- Show an orange	Theme- Uses for pumpkins Letter Skills-Sing Alphabet song Math Skills- Pumpkin Patch Counting Color/Shape- Play I Spy	Theme- What's in a pumpkin Letter Skills-Erase the letter Math Skills- Flashlight Writing Color/Shape-Stand up if you have on __ game	Theme-Taste test Letter Skills-Pick a Pocket Math Skills- Who Has # __game Color/Shape-review with flashcards	L D T R I P
Story Time	Read book:	Read book:	Read book:	Read book:	
Game Time/Music	Music – Colorful Shakers	Game - Pumpkin Patch Picking	Music – "Alphabats" Song	Game - Ring the Pumpkin Bucket game	Suggestions: Visit pumpkin patch Carve pumpkin together Have a Fall Festival
Closing Circle	Review today's theme, letter and math skills, color and shape	Review today's theme, letter and math skills, color and shape	Review today's theme, letter and math skills, color and shape	Review today's theme, letter and math skills, color and shape	Review this week's theme, letter, math, color, shape Pass out Care Bear backpack & Star Student briefcase

Weekly Lesson Plan   Theme: Community Helpers

Letter: H   Number: 3   Scripture:
Color: yellow   Shape: rectangle   Gal. 5:13

Small Group Time:
1.Letter Skills
2.Numbers/Readiness Skills
3-Art or Cooking

	Monday	Tuesday	Wednesday	Thursday	Friday
Bible Time	Read Bible verse Tell Story of Jesus Feeds 5000	Review Bible verse Prayer Time (use small white board to record/erase requests and praises)	Review Bible verse Prayer Time	Review Bible verse Prayer Time	Review Bible story Review Bible verse Prayer Time
Greeting Circle	Star Student Read Care Bear Journal Class Jobs Calendar/Weather Routine Birthdays & Share Bears (4)	Good Morning song Calendar/Weather Routine Birthdays Share Bears (4)	Good Morning song Calendar/Weather Routine Birthdays Share Bears (4)	Good Morning song Calendar/Weather Routine Birthdays Share Bears (4)	Good Morning song Calendar/Weather Routine Birthdays Share Bears (4)
Center Time/ Small Group Time	1. Decorate blank H with happy face stickers 2. Barber Shop Writing 3. Fireman Finger Painting	1.Hammer H's 2. Police Fingerprints 3.Doctor Collage	1.Letter H Hunt 2. Firetruck Wheel Sorting 3.Toothbrush painting	1.no activity today 2.Cotton ball counting 3.Cooking: Decorate cookies	F I E
Circle Time	Theme- What are Community Helpers? Letter Skills-Intro. letter Math Skills-Intro. number 3 Color/Shape-Disc. yellow, rectangle	Theme-Garbage Collector Letter Skills-H says "h" like hat Math Skills- Baker's blueberry pancakes game Color/Shape-How many rectangles can we find?	Theme-Doctor Letter Skills- Happy Face Stickers Math Skills- 3's Concept practice Color/Shape-Yellow-Hunt w/ glasses	Theme-Review Letter Skills-Review Math Skills-Review Color/Shape-Review	L D T
Story Time	Read book:	Read book:	Read book:	Read book:	R I P
Game Time/Music	Game-Garbage Man game	Music-Johnny Works with 1 Hammer	Game-Stop Drop and Roll	Game-Fire Brigade game	Suggestions; Fire Department Police Station Post Office
Closing Circle	Review today's theme, letter and math skills, color and shape	Review today's theme, letter and math skills, color and shape	Review today's theme, letter and math skills, color and shape	Review today's theme, letter and math skills, color and shape	Review this week's theme, letter, math, color, shape Pass out Care Bear backpack & Star Student briefcase

Weekly Lesson Plan   Theme: Indians

Letter: I   Number: 3   Scripture:
Color: yellow   Shape: rectangle Gal. 5:25

Small GroupTime:
1. Letter Skills
2. Numbers/Readiness Skills
3- Art or Cooking

	Monday	Tuesday	Wednesday	Thursday	Friday
Bible Time	Read Bible verse Tell Story of Jesus Feeds 5000	Review Bible verse Prayer Time (use small white board to record/erase requests and praises)	Review Bible verse Prayer Time	Review Bible verse Prayer Time	Review Bible story Review Bible verse Prayer Time
Greeting Circle	Star Student Read Care Bear Journal Class Jobs Calendar/Weather Routine Birthdays & Share Bears (4)	Good Morning song Calendar/Weather Routine Birthdays Share Bears (4)	Good Morning song Calendar/Weather Routine Birthdays Share Bears (4)	Good Morning song Calendar/Weather Routine Birthdays Share Bears (4)	Good Morning song Calendar/Weather Routine Birthdays Share Bears (4)
Center Time/ Small Group Time	1. Decorate blank I with "itchy dots" 2. Indian necklace-string noodles 3. Indian vests	1. Add feather to head-dress 2. Cover #3 with stickers 3. Indian clamp bracelets	1. Indian Corn Napkin rings (Shapes) 2. Feather painting (Color) 3. Corn Painting	1. 2. Indian headband (Art) 3. Cooking: Make cornbread muffins	F I E
Circle Time	Theme- Indians used pictures Letter Skills-Intro. letter I, I Math Skills-Disc. number 3 Color/Shape-Disc. yellow, rectangle	Theme-Disc. where Indians lived Letter Skills-"Itchy spots" game Math Skills- One Little, Two Little...Indians song Color/Shape-Show banana (yellow)	Theme-Disc. what Indians wore Letter Skills- Add feathers to headdress Math Skills- Row your canoe Color/Shape-	Theme-Disc. what Indians ate Letter Skills-Letter I box Math Skills-Review Color/Shape-Review	L D T R I P
Story Time	Read book:	Read book:	Read book:	Read book:	
Game Time/Music	Game-Picking Lemons (yellow)	Music-Popcorn	Game-Play with feathers (keep in the air)	Music-Pass the feather	Suggestions: Watch moviePocahontas Indian museum Native American guest
Closing Circle	Review today's theme, letter and math skills, color and shape	Review today's theme, letter and math skills, color and shape	Review today's theme, letter and math skills, color and shape	Review today's theme, letter and math skills, color and shape	Review this week's theme, letter, math, color, shape Pass out Care Bear backpack & Star Student briefcase

Weekly Lesson Plan

Theme: Special Holiday: Thanksgiving

Letter: review
Color: yellow
Number: review
Shape: rectangle

Scripture: 1 Chro. 29:13

Small Group Time:
1. Letter Skills
2. Numbers/Readiness Skills
3- Art or Cooking

	Monday	Tuesday	Wednesday	Thursday	Friday
Bible Time	Read Bible verse Tell Story of The One Thankful Leper	Review Bible verse Prayer Time (use small white board to record/erase requests and praises)	Review Bible verse Prayer Time	Review Bible verse Prayer Time	Review Bible story Review Bible verse Prayer Time
Greeting Circle	Star Student Read Care Bear Journal Class Jobs Calendar/Weather Routine Birthdays & Share Bears (4)	Good Morning song Calendar/Weather Routine Birthdays Share Bears (4)	Good Morning song Calendar/Weather Routine Birthdays Share Bears (4)	Good Morning song Calendar/Weather Routine Birthdays Share Bears (4)	Good Morning song Calendar/Weather Routine Birthdays Share Bears (4)
Center Time/ Small Group Time	1. Trace alphabet magnets 2. no activity today 3. Turkey Placemat	1. Alphabet stamping 2. Indian Vest (see Art) 3. Thanksgiving Candle	1. Playdough with alphabet cookie cutters 2. Finish Indian Vests (see Art) 3. Paper Bag Turkey	1. no activity today 2. Paper Plate Collage (see Art) 3. Cooking: Sugar Waffle cone Cornucopia	F I E L D T R I P
Circle Time	Theme- First Thanksgiving - Pilgrims Letter Skills-What's the Sound song Math Skills-What Comes After game Color/Shape- Jump On Color game	Theme- First Thanksgiving - Indians Letter Skills-Sing Alphabet song Math Skills- Fishing for Numbers Color/Shape- Play I Spy	Theme- First Thanksgiving - Feast Letter Skills-Erase the letter Math Skills- Flashlight Writing Color/Shape-Stand up if you have on __ game	Theme-Thanksgiving Today Letter Skills-Pick a Pocket Math Skills- Who Has # __ game Color/Shape-review with flashcards	
Story Time	Read book:	Read book:	Read book:	Read book:	
Game Time/Music	Music - Turkey Pokey	Music - Apple Pie Tamborines	Game - Turkey Bean Bag Toss	Music - Dinner Bells	Suggestions: Have parents come for Thanksgiving Meal
Closing Circle	Review today's theme, letter and math skills, color and shape	Review today's theme, letter and math skills, color and shape	Review today's theme, letter and math skills, color and shape	Review today's theme, letter and math skills, color and shape	Review this week's theme, letter, math, color, shape Pass out Care Bear backpack & Star Student briefcase

Weekly Lesson Plan   Theme: Jungle Safari

| | Letter: J | Color: green | Number: 4 | Shape: triangle | Scripture: Mttw: 28:20 |

Small GroupTime:
1.Letter Skills
2.Numbers/Readiness Skills
3-Art or Cooking

	Monday	Tuesday	Wednesday	Thursday	Friday
Bible Time	Read Bible verse Tell Story of Moses in the basket	Review Bible verse Prayer Time (use small white board to record/erase requests and praises)	Review Bible verse Prayer Time	Review Bible verse Prayer Time	Review Bible story Review Bible verse Prayer Time
Greeting Circle	Star Student Read Care Bear Journal Class Jobs Calendar/Weather Routine Birthdays & Share Bears (4)	Good Morning song Calendar/Weather Routine Birthdays Share Bears (4)	Good Morning song Calendar/Weather Routine Birthdays Share Bears (4)	Good Morning song Calendar/Weather Routine Birthdays Share Bears (4)	Good Morning song Calendar/Weather Routine Birthdays Share Bears (4)
Center Time/ Small Group Time	1. Decorate blank J with jewels 2. Make 4 with popsicle sticks 3. Safari binoculars	1.Letter J Hunt 2.Dry erase board practice 3.Yarn lion stick puppet	1.Jewlery Relay (see Games) 2. Number 4 ...with stickers 3.Scizzor Skills Snake	1.Jungle Trip (see Games) 2.Safari triangle hunt 3.Cooking:Monkey Bananas	F I E L D T R I P
Circle Time	Theme-Disc. Jungle-show Africa Letter Skills-Intro. letter J,j Math Skills-Intro. number 4 Color/Shape-Disc. green, triangle	Theme-Disc. what jungle looks like Letter Skills-J says "J" like jump game Math Skills- Repeat patterns for 4 Color/Shape-Make a list of as many green things as you can	Theme-Disc. animals that live in jungle Letter Skills-Add Ants to Anthill game Math Skills- Number Jump game Color/Shape-Triangle hunt	Theme-Disc. where animals live Letter Skills-J like a Jellyfish game Math Skills- Four Corners game Color/Shape-Walk Around the Triangle	
Story Time	Read book:	Read book:	Read book:	Read book:	
Game Time/Music	Game- Jump on J's	Music – Move like a ___	Game – Hot Monkey (like Hot Potato)	Game – Lion Says (like Simon Says)	Suggestions: Watch movie "The Jungle Book" or watch, "Go Diego, Go"
Closing Circle	Review today's theme, letter and math skills, color and shape	Review today's theme, letter and math skills, color and shape	Review today's theme, letter and math skills, color and shape	Review today's theme, letter and math skills, color and shape	Review this week's theme, letter, math, color, shape Pass out Care Bear backpack & Star Student briefcase

Weekly Lesson Plan Theme: Special Holiday: Christmas

		Letter: review	Number: review	Scripture:
		Color: green	Shape: triangle	Luke 2:11

Small Group Time:
1. Letter Skills
2. Numbers/Readiness Skills
3-Art or Cooking

	Monday	Tuesday	Wednesday	Thursday	Friday
Bible Time	Read Bible verse Tell Story of Jesus' Birth	Review Bible verse Prayer Time (use small white board to record/erase requests and praises)	Review Bible verse Prayer Time	Review Bible verse Prayer Time	Review Bible story Review Bible verse Prayer Time
Greeting Circle	Star Student Read Care Bear Journal Class Jobs Calendar/Weather Routine Birthdays & Share Bears (4)	Good Morning song Calendar/Weather Routine Birthdays Share Bears (4)	Good Morning song Calendar/Weather Routine Birthdays Share Bears (4)	Good Morning song Calendar/Weather Routine Birthdays Share Bears (4)	Good Morning song Calendar/Weather Routine Birthdays Share Bears (4)
Center Time/ Small Group Time	1. Trace alphabet magnets 2. no activity today 3. Christmas Reindeer Bookmark and Candy Cane (see Gift section)	1. Alphabet stamping 2. no activity today 3. Christmas Crayons (see Gift section)	1. Playdough with alphabet cookie cutters 2. no activity today 3. Pine Cone Tree (see Art)	1. no activity today 2. Handprint Santa 3. Cooking: Decorate Christmas Cookies	F I E
Circle Time	Theme- The First Christmas-Jesus' Birth Letter Skills-What's the Sound song Math Skills-What Comes After game Color/Shape- Jump On Color game	Theme- The First Christmas - Shepherds Visit Letter Skills-Sing Alphabet song Math Skills- Fishing for Numbers Color/Shape- Play I Spy	Theme- The First Christmas-Wise Men Visit Later Letter Skills-Erase the letter Math Skills- Flashlight Writing Color/Shape-Stand up if you have on game	Theme-Christmas Traditions Today Letter Skills-Pick a Pocket Math Skills- Who Has # __ game Color/Shape-review with flashcards	L D T R I P
Story Time	Read book:	Read book:	Read book:	Read book:	
Game Time/Music	Music – Jingle Bells	Game – Christmas Balloons	Music – Sing Favorite Christmas Carols	Music – Sing Favorite Christmas Carols	Suggestions: Visit Nursing Home and sing carols Happy Birthday Jesus Party
Closing Circle	Review today's theme, letter and math skills, color and shape	Review today's theme, letter and math skills, color and shape	Review today's theme, letter and math skills, color and shape	Review today's theme, letter and math skills, color and shape	Review this week's theme, letter, math, color, shape Pass out Care Bear backpack & Star Student briefcase

Weekly Lesson Plan   Theme: Kings, Queens, and Castles

Letter: K Color: blue Number: 5 Shape: star Scripture: Luke 12:34

Small Group Time:
1. Letter Skills
2. Numbers/Readiness Skills
3. Art or Cooking

	Monday	Tuesday	Wednesday	Thursday	Friday
Bible Time	Read Bible verse Tell Story of the Armor of God	Review Bible verse Prayer Time (use small white board to record/erase requests and praises)	Review Bible verse Prayer Time	Review Bible verse Prayer Time	Review Bible story Review Bible verse Prayer Time
Greeting Circle	Star Student Read Care Bear Journal Class Jobs Calendar/Weather Routine Birthdays & Share Bears (4)	Good Morning song Calendar/Weather Routine Birthdays Share Bears (4)	Good Morning song Calendar/Weather Routine Birthdays Share Bears (4)	Good Morning song Calendar/Weather Routine Birthdays Share Bears (4)	Good Morning song Calendar/Weather Routine Birthdays Share Bears (4)
Center Time/ Small Group Time	1. Decorate blank K with kisses 2. King's chest counting 3. Make King/Queen crown	1. Letter K box 2. Stringing necklaces 3. Play with blue playdough that has glitter (see Color)	1. K kangaroo pocket collection 2. Measure a Giant activ. 3. Star Wands	1. K is for Kiss picture 2. Shining Stars (see Shapes) 3. Knight's helmet	F I E
Circle Time	Theme-What did kings/queens do? Letter Skills- Introduce Letter K Math Skills-Intro. number 5 Color/Shape-Intro. blue/star	Theme-What did kings/queens wear? Letter Skills-K like Kangaroo game Math Skills- Count fingers(see Math) Color/Shape-Star stickers	Theme-What did kings/queens eat? Letter Skills- Add Jewels to crown game (see Letters) Math Skills- Give me five Color/Shape-Sing Twinkle, Twinkle	Theme- Where did kings/queens live? Letter Skills-K is for Kiss game Math Skills-5 Happy Kings fingerplay Color/Shape-Starry Night Search	L D T
Story Time	Read book:	Read book:	Read book:	Read book:	R I P
Game Time/Music	Game - King/Queen May I	Music-Key Jiggling	Game - King/Queen Says (like Simon Says)	Music – Jump inside the Moat	Suggestions: Watch The Lion King
Closing Circle	Review today's theme, letter and math skills, color and shape	Review today's theme, letter and math skills, color and shape	Review today's theme, letter and math skills, color and shape	Review today's theme, letter and math skills, color and shape	Review this week's theme, letter, math, color, shape Pass out Care Bear backpack & Star Student briefcase

Weekly Lesson Plan — Theme: Library and Books

Letter: L Color: blue Number: 5 Shape: star Scripture: Ps. 119:130

Small Group Time:
1. Letter Skills
2. Numbers/Readiness Skills
3. Art or Cooking

	Monday	Tuesday	Wednesday	Thursday	Friday
Bible Time	Read Bible verse; Tell Story Jesus Heals a Blind Man	Review Bible verse; Prayer Time (use small white board to record/erase requests and praises)	Review Bible verse; Prayer Time	Review Bible verse; Prayer Time	Review Bible story; Review Bible verse; Prayer Time
Greeting Circle	Star Student; Read Care Bear Journal; Class Jobs; Calendar/Weather Routine; Birthdays & Share Bears (4)	Good Morning song; Calendar/Weather Routine; Birthdays; Share Bears (4)	Good Morning song; Calendar/Weather Routine; Birthdays; Share Bears (4)	Good Morning song; Calendar/Weather Routine; Birthdays; Share Bears (4)	Good Morning song; Calendar/Weather Routine; Birthdays; Share Bears (4)
Center Time/ Small Group Time	1. Decorate blank L with leaves 2. 3. Star Frame (see Shapes)	1. Make a Letter L book 2. Lucky Charms sorting 3. Lucky Charms stars (see Shapes)	1. 2. Goldfish Counting 3. Playdough/star cookie cutters (see Shapes)	1. no activity today 2. Ladybug Counting 3. Cooking: Letter L biscuits	F I E / L D / T / R I P
Circle Time	Theme- Read: Corduroy goes to the Library; Letter Skills- Intro. Letter L; Math Skills-Leaf Toss; Color/Shape-Blue Match	Theme- Discuss what's in a library; Letter Skills-Lollipop activity; Math Skills- Count the books; Color/Shape-Am I blue2 (see Color)	Theme-Discuss fiction/nonfiction; Letter Skills- Leaf activity; Math Skills-Repeat the Pattern; Color/Shape-Look for Blue's Clues	Theme- Disc. library card; Letter Skills-Letter L box; Math Skills-; Color/Shape-Seeing Stars (see Shape)	
Story Time	Read book:	Read book:	Read book:	Read book:	
Game Time/Music	Game – Book Relay	Music – Bremen Town Muscians	Music - Quiet music and books	Favorite books - let children bring favorite book from home; read each one to the class during this time	Suggestions: Visit your town's library
Closing Circle	Review today's theme, letter and math skills, color and shape	Review today's theme, letter and math skills, color and shape	Review today's theme, letter and math skills, color and shape	Review today's theme, letter and math skills, color and shape	Review this week's theme, letter, math, color, shape; Pass out Care Bear backpack & Star Student briefcase

Weekly Lesson Plan — Theme: Mittens

Letter: M   Number: 5   Scripture:
Color: blue   Shape: star   1 Thes. 5:17

	Monday	Tuesday	Wednesday	Thursday	Friday
Bible Time	Read Bible verse. Tell Story of Mary and Martha	Review Bible verse. Prayer Time (use small white board to record/erase requests and praises)	Review Bible verse. Prayer Time	Review Bible verse. Prayer Time	Review Bible story. Review Bible verse. Prayer Time
Greeting Circle	Star Student. Read Care Bear Journal. Class Jobs. Calendar/Weather Routine. Birthdays & Share Bears (4)	Good Morning song. Calendar/Weather Routine. Birthdays. Share Bears (4)	Good Morning song. Calendar/Weather Routine. Birthdays. Share Bears (4)	Good Morning song. Calendar/Weather Routine. Birthdays. Share Bears (4)	Good Morning song. Calendar/Weather Routine. Birthdays. Share Bears (4)
Center Time/ Small Group Time	1. Decorate blank M with colorful markers. 2. Yarn Mitten counting. 3. Mitten decorating	1.M is for Mountain. 2.Write #5 with ice. 3.Shiny Star Playdough (see Shape)	1.Mitten Lacing. 2.Count the Points & add tin foil(see Shape). 3.no activity today	1.no activity today. 2.Mitten Match. 3.Cooking-Marshmallow Snowman	F I E
Circle Time	Theme- Read The Mitten by Jan Brett. Letter Skills-Introduce Letter M. Math Skills-Ice Fishing for Numbers. Color/Shape-Compare mitten with star	Theme-Discuss animals in book. Letter Skills-Mitten on clothesline game. Math Skills- Counting Snowballs. Color/Shape-Find the Blue Mitten	Theme-Discuss animals in winter. Letter Skills-. Math Skills- 5 Little Mittens fingerplay. Color/Shape- sing Twinkle, Twinkle Little Star	Theme- Mittens Matter hot/cold experiment. Letter Skills-Letter M box. Math Skills- Mitten Pretend. Color/Shape-Mitten Hide and Seek	L D T
Story Time	Read book:	Read book:	Read book:	Read book:	R I P
Game Time/Music	Game - Kittens Lost Mittens game	Game - Dress Up Relay	Game - Shaving Creme Snow	Game - Mitten Toss	Suggestions: Knitting Guest. Visit Farm-sheep
Closing Circle	Review today's theme, letter and math skills, color and shape	Review today's theme, letter and math skills, color and shape	Review today's theme, letter and math skills, color and shape	Review today's theme, letter and math skills, color and shape	Review this week's theme, letter, math, color, shape. Pass out Care Bear backpack & Star Student briefcase

Weekly Lesson Plan Theme: Nutrition and Health

Small Group Time:
1. Letter Skills
2. Numbers/Readiness Skills
3. Art or Cooking

	Monday	Tuesday	Wednesday	Thursday	Friday
Bible Time	Read Bible verse Tell Story of The Prodigal Son	Review Bible verse Prayer Time (use small white board to record/erase requests and praises)	Review Bible verse Prayer Time	Review Bible verse Prayer Time	Review Bible story Review Bible verse Prayer Time
Greeting Circle	Star Student Read Care Bear Journal Class Jobs Calendar/Weather Routine Birthdays & Share Bears (4)	Good Morning song Calendar/Weather Routine Birthdays Share Bears (4)	Good Morning song Calendar/Weather Routine Birthdays Share Bears (4)	Good Morning song Calendar/Weather Routine Birthdays Share Bears (4)	Good Morning song Calendar/Weather Routine Birthdays Share Bears (4)
Center Time/ Small Group Time	1. Decorate blank N with nest (wheat cereal) 2. Color Sorting (see Color) 3. Food pyramid (or plate)	1. N is for Numbers collage 2. Meal Sorting (see Math) 3. Food Stamping	1. N is for Necktie 2. Playdough Baking (Shape) 3. Paper Plate Healthy Lunch collage	1. no activity today 2. Muffin Tin Sorting (Color) 3. Cooking: Trail Mix	F I E L D T R I P
Circle Time	Theme- Discuss the 5 Food Groups Letter Skills-Intro. letter N Math Skills-Baking and Counting Color/Shape-5 Star Restaurants (see Shape)	Theme-Discuss Fruits/Vegetables Letter Skills-N is like a nest game Math Skills- Counting apples Color/Shape-Muffin Flashcards (see Color)	Theme-Discuss Grains Letter Skills-Pin the Nose on the Baker Math Skills- Pretzel Counting Color/Shape- Pretzel Star	Theme- Discuss Protein & Dairy Letter Skills-Nest/Baby Bird Math Skills- Give Me Five Color/Shape-repeat Muffin Flashcards activ. (see Color)	
Story Time	Read book:	Read book:	Read book:	Read book:	
Game Time/Music	Music - Bean Maracas	Music - "Old MacDonald" garden version	Game - Excercise	Music - Bean Maracas	Suggestions: Farmer's Market Pizza Chain Grocery Store
Closing Circle	Review today's theme, letter and math skills, color and shape	Review today's theme, letter and math skills, color and shape	Review today's theme, letter and math skills, color and shape	Review today's theme, letter and math skills, color and shape	Review this week's theme, letter, math, color, shape Pass out Care Bear backpack & Star Student briefcase

Weekly Lesson Plan — Theme: Ocean

Small Group Time:
1. Letter Skills
2. Numbers/Readiness Skills
3-Art or Cooking

	Monday	Tuesday	Wednesday	Thursday	Friday
Bible Time	Read Bible verse Tell Story of The Great Catch	Review Bible verse Prayer Time (use small white board to record/erase requests and praises)	Review Bible verse Prayer Time	Review Bible verse Prayer Time	Review Bible story Review Bible verse Prayer Time
Greeting Circle	Star Student Read Care Bear Journal Class Jobs Calendar/Weather Routine Birthdays & Share Bears (4)	Good Morning song Calendar/Weather Routine Birthdays Share Bears (4)	Good Morning song Calendar/Weather Routine Birthdays Share Bears (4)	Good Morning song Calendar/Weather Routine Birthdays Share Bears (4)	Good Morning song Calendar/Weather Routine Birthdays Share Bears (4)
Center Time/ Small Group Time	1. Decorate blank O with Cheerios 2. Number 6 Hermit Crab Shell 3. Ocean in a Bottle	1. O is for Octopus 2. Sea Shell Counters (see Math) 3. Fish With Scales	1. Sand Writing (O & 6) 2. Heart Fish (see Shape) 3. Paper Plate Jellyfish	1. no activity today 2. Red and White make pink (see Color) 3. Cooking: Sand Pudding	F I E L D T R I P
Circle Time	Theme- Discuss 5 major oceans Letter Skills-Intro. letter O Math Skills-Intro. number 6 Color/Shape- Intro. pink/heart	Theme-Discuss salt water Letter Skills- "Ahhhh" game Math Skills- Count Sea Shells Color/Shape-Make a list of pink things	Theme-Discuss fish in the ocean Letter Skills- Discuss long O sound Math Skills- Number Diving Color/Shape-Heart Exchange	Theme- Other creatures in the ocean Letter Skills-Letter O box Math Skills- Caught a Shark Alive Color/Shape-Demonstrate red/white make pink	
Story Time	Read book:	Read book:	Read book:	Read book:	
Game Time/Music	Game - Beach Ball Bowling	Game - Kiddie Pool Playground	Game - Swim in the Ocean	Music – Rainsticks	Suggestions: Watch the movie "Nemo" Visit an aquarium Visit petstore with fish
Closing Circle	Review today's theme, letter and math skills, color and shape	Review today's theme, letter and math skills, color and shape	Review today's theme, letter and math skills, color and shape	Review today's theme, letter and math skills, color and shape	Review this week's theme, letter, math, color, shape Pass out Care Bear backpack & Star Student briefcase

Weekly Lesson Plan   Theme: Plants

Letter: P   Number: 6   Scripture:
Color: pink   Shape: heart   Gen. 1:11

Small Group Time:
1.Letter Skills
2.Numbers/Readiness Skills
3-Art or Cooking

	Monday	Tuesday	Wednesday	Thursday	Friday
Bible Time	Read Bible verse Tell Story of Creation	Review Bible verse Prayer Time (use small white board to record/erase requests and praises)	Review Bible verse Prayer Time	Review Bible verse Prayer Time	Review Bible story Review Bible verse Prayer Time
Greeting Circle	Star Student Read Care Bear Journal Class Jobs Calendar/Weather Routine Birthdays & Share Bears (4)	Good Morning song Calendar/Weather Routine Birthdays Share Bears (4)	Good Morning song Calendar/Weather Routine Birthdays Share Bears (4)	Good Morning song Calendar/Weather Routine Birthdays Share Bears (4)	Good Morning song Calendar/Weather Routine Birthdays Share Bears (4)
Center Time/ Small Group Time	1. Decorate blank P with polka dots 2. Seed Sorting 3. Paper Cup Head with Grass Hair	1.P Popcorn Picture 2.Seed Packet Match 3.Grow a potato	1.Letter P collage 2.Index Card Flashcards 3.Terra Cotta Pots (for use as Valentine's Day gift for parents)	1.no activity today 2.Flour Hearts 3.Cooking: Dirt Pie	F I E L D T R I P
Circle Time	Theme- Disc. what plants need Letter Skills-Intro. letter P Math Skills-Flower Counting Color/Shape-Heart Search	Theme-Disc. seeds Letter Skills- P says "p" like puff of air (bubbles game) Math Skills- Color/Shape-Draw a heart with finger	Theme-Disc. soil/dirt & water Letter Skills- P like popcorn Math Skills- Use one set of seed flashcards to review numbers together-made during Center Time. Color/Shape-	Theme- Disc. roots/carbon dioxide Letter Skills-Letter P box Math Skills- Roll the Dice Color/Shape-Heart Burn game	
Story Time	Read book:	Read book:	Read book:	Read book:	
Game Time/Music	Music – Streamers	Game – Act out growing from seed to plant	Music – Sand Paper Blocks	Game – Water Play	Suggestions: Visit a nursery Plant garden outside
Closing Circle	Review today's theme, letter and math skills, color and shape	Review today's theme, letter and math skills, color and shape	Review today's theme, letter and math skills, color and shape	Review today's theme, letter and math skills, color and shape	Review this week's theme, letter, math, color, shape Pass out Care Bear backpack & Star Student briefcase

Weekly Lesson Plan

Theme: Special Holiday: Valentines Week

Small Group Time:
1. Letter Skills
2. Numbers/Readiness Skills
3- Art or Cooking

Letter: review   Number: review   Scripture:
Color: pink   Shape: heart   John 13:34

	Monday	Tuesday	Wednesday	Thursday	Friday
Bible Time	Read Bible verse Tell Story of The Good Samaritan	Review Bible verse Prayer Time (use small white board to record/erase requests and praises)	Review Bible verse Prayer Time	Review Bible verse Prayer Time	Review Bible story Review Bible verse Prayer Time
Greeting Circle	Star Student Read Care Bear Journal Class Jobs Calendar/Weather Routine Birthdays & Share Bears (4)	Good Morning song Calendar/Weather Routine Birthdays Share Bears (4)	Good Morning song Calendar/Weather Routine Birthdays Share Bears (4)	Good Morning song Calendar/Weather Routine Birthdays Share Bears (4)	Good Morning song Calendar/Weather Routine Birthdays Share Bears (4)
Center Time/ Small Group Time	1. Trace alphabet magnets 2. no activity today 3. Valentine Card Bucket (see Art)	1. Alphabet stamping 2. Stained Glass Heart hanging (see Color) 3. no activity today	1. Playdough with alphabet cookie cutters 2. no activity today 3. Sweet Breakfast Treat (see Gift Ideas section)	1. no activity today 2. make Valentine cards 3. Cooking: Cupcake Decorating	F I E L D T R I P
Circle Time	Theme- Who Was Saint Valentine? Letter Skills-What's the Sound song Math Skills-What Comes After game Color/Shape- Jump On Color game	Theme- Who Do You Love? Letter Skills-Sing Alphabet song Math Skills- Fishing for Numbers Color/Shape-Play I Spy	Theme-Valentine Traditions Letter Skills-Erase the letter Math Skills- Flash light Writing Color/Shape-Stand up if you have on ___ game	Theme-Valentine Cards Letter Skills-Pick a Pocket Math Skills- Who Has #__ game Color/Shape-review with flashcards	
Story Time	Read book:	Read book:	Read book:	Read book:	
Game Time/Music	Music – Sign Language "I Love You" and "Jesus Loves Me"	Game – A Tisket A Tasket	Game - Valentine Bingo	Game – Who Stole My Heart? game	Suggestions: Visit Nursing Home and take Valentine Cards Have a Valentine Party
Closing Circle	Review today's theme, letter and math skills, color and shape	Review today's theme, letter and math skills, color and shape	Review today's theme, letter and math skills, color and shape	Review today's theme, letter and math skills, color and shape	Review this week's theme, letter, math, color, shape Pass out Care Bear backpack & Star Student briefcase

Weekly Lesson Plan — Theme: Reduce, Reuse, Recycle

Letter: R   Number: 7   Scripture:
Color: white   Shape: diamond Rom. 12:21

Small Group Time:
1-Letter Skills
2-Numbers/Readiness Skills
3-Art or Cooking

	Monday	Tuesday	Wednesday	Thursday	Friday
Bible Time	Read Bible verse Tell Story of Paul	Review Bible verse Prayer Time (use small white board to record/erase requests and praises)	Review Bible verse Prayer Time	Review Bible verse Prayer Time	Review Bible story Review Bible verse Prayer Time
Greeting Circle	Star Student Read Care Bear Journal Class Jobs Calendar/Weather Routine Birthdays & Share Bears (4)	Good Morning song Calendar/Weather Routine Birthdays Share Bears (4)	Good Morning song Calendar/Weather Routine Birthdays Share Bears (4)	Good Morning song Calendar/Weather Routine Birthdays Share Bears (4)	Good Morning song Calendar/Weather Routine Birthdays Share Bears (4)
Center/ Small Group Time	1. Decorate blank R with rice 2. White pencil can (see Color) 3. Sock hand puppet	1. R is for Rainbow 2. Birthday Cake Candle Counting 3. Lid Birdfeeder	1. Find the R's 2. Cereal Box Puzzles 3. Christmas card puzzles	1. no activity today 2. White Chalk Picture (see Color) 3. Cooking: Earth Cupcake	F I E
Circle Time	Theme- What does reduce, reuse, recycle mean? Letter Skills-Intro. letter R Math Skills-Intro. number 7 Color/Shape- Intro. white/diamond	Theme-Discuss: Recycling Center Letter Skills- Roll the Ball game Math Skills- Recycled Wind Chime Color/Shape-I Spy a Diamond	Theme-Discuss: Landfills Letter Skills- R is for Red Math Skills- Birthday Cake Counting Color/Shape-Make a list of white things	Theme- Discuss: Composting Letter Skills- Letter R box Math Skills- Recycling Saves Money Counting game Color/Shape- Color Flashcards	L D T R I P
Story Time	Read book:	Read book:	Read book:	Read book:	
Game Time/Music	Game – Pick Up Trash	Game - Soda Bottle Bowling	Game - Refrigerator Box Tunnel	Music - Kazoo	Suggestions: Visit local Recycling Center Watch movie-A Bug's Life
Closing Circle	Review today's theme, letter and math skills, color and shape	Review today's theme, letter and math skills, color and shape	Review today's theme, letter and math skills, color and shape	Review today's theme, letter and math skills, color and shape	Review this week's theme, letter, math, color, shape Pass out Care Bear backpack & Star Student briefcase

Weekly Lesson Plan — Theme: Quack Like a Duck

Small Group Time:
1. Letter Skills
2. Numbers/Readiness Skills
3-Art or Cooking

Letter: Q
Color: pink
Number: 6
Shape: heart
Scripture: Mttw. 6:14

	Monday	Tuesday	Wednesday	Thursday	Friday
Bible Time	Read Bible verse / Tell Story of Joseph and the Coat of Many Colors	Review Bible verse / Prayer Time (use small white board to record/erase requests and praises)	Review Bible verse / Prayer Time	Review Bible verse / Prayer Time	Review Bible story / Review Bible verse / Prayer Time
Greeting Circle	Star Student / Read Care Bear Journal / Class Jobs / Calendar/Weather Routine / Birthdays & Share Bears (4)	Good Morning song / Calendar/Weather Routine / Birthdays / Share Bears (4)	Good Morning song / Calendar/Weather Routine / Birthdays / Share Bears (4)	Good Morning song / Calendar/Weather Routine / Birthdays / Share Bears (4)	Good Morning song / Calendar/Weather Routine / Birthdays / Share Bears (4)
Center Time/ Small Group Time	1. Decorate blank Q with quilt squares / 2. Shape Duck (see Shape) / 3. Paint with feathers	1. Q is for Q tips / 2. Playdough with heart cookie cutters (see Shape) / 3. Duckling Footprings	1. Q is for Quack picture / 2. Candy Box Tracing (see Shape) / 3. Paper Plate Duck	1. no activity today / 2. Fruit Loop Sorting / 3. Cooking: Strawberry Milkshakes (pink)	F I E
Circle Time	Theme- Read Make Way for Ducklings by Robert McCloskey; discuss what ducks look like / Letter Skills-Intro. letter Q / Math Skills-Pick up Ducks game / Color/Shape-	Theme-Disc. what ducks eat / Letter Skills- Roll on Quilt game / Math Skills- 6 Little Ducks song / Color/Shape-Pink Cotton Candy (see Color)	Theme-Disc. duck flying formation / Letter Skills- Q llke Quick game / Math Skills- Number Flashcards / Color/Shape-Pink Pokey	Theme- Disc. where ducks live / Letter Skills- Letter Q box / Math Skills- 6 Seconds game / Color/Shape- Repeat Pink Pokey (add other colors as a review)	L D T R I P
Story Time	Read book:	Read book:	Read book:	Read book:	
Game Time/Music	Music - Waddle like a Duck	Game - Dunk the Ducks	Music - Egg Shakers	Game - Duck, Duck , Goose	Suggestions: / Visit a pond / Watch Charlotte's Web / Have farmer bring in ducks
Closing Circle	Review today's theme, letter and math skills, color and shape	Review today's theme, letter and math skills, color and shape	Review today's theme, letter and math skills, color and shape	Review today's theme, letter and math skills, color and shape	Review this week's theme, letter, math, color, shape / Pass out Care Bear backpack & Star Student briefcase

Weekly Lesson Plan   Theme: Senses (My Five Senses)

Small Group Time:
1. Letter Skills
2. Numbers/Readiness Skills
3-Art or Cooking

Letter: S   Number: 7   Scripture:
Color: white   Shape: diamond   Prov. 20:12

	Monday	Tuesday	Wednesday	Thursday	Friday
Bible Time	Read Bible verse Tell Story of Jesus at the Temple	Review Bible verse Prayer Time (use small white board to record/erase requests and praises)	Review Bible verse Prayer Time	Review Bible verse Prayer Time	Review Bible story Review Bible verse Prayer Time
Greeting Circle	Star Student Read Care Bear Journal Class Jobs Calendar/Weather Routine Birthdays & Share Bears (4)	Good Morning song Calendar/Weather Routine Birthdays Share Bears (4)	Good Morning song Calendar/Weather Routine Birthdays Share Bears (4)	Good Morning song Calendar/Weather Routine Birthdays Share Bears (4)	Good Morning song Calendar/Weather Routine Birthdays Share Bears (4)
Center Time/ Small Group Time	1. Decorate blank S with string 2. M & M Counting 3. Hand Collage (touch)	1.S is for Smelly Flower 2. Diamond Stamping (see Shape) 3.Gingerbread Man (smell)	1. S is for Sound 2. Homemade Playdough (see Color) 3. Beet Painting (taste)	1.S is for Sight Collage 2. no activity for today 3. Cooking: Jello Jigglers	F I E L D T R I P
Circle Time	Theme- Intro. 5 Senses Letter Skills-Intro. Letter S Math Skills-Counting Sheep game Color/Shape- Look for White	Theme- Mystery Touch Box Letter Skills- S like a snake game Math Skills-7 Silly Snakes rhyme Color/Shape-Diamond like a Square	Theme-Taste Test Letter Skills- Hot Snake game Math Skills- Number 7 Stomp Color/Shape-Diamond Mining	Theme-Hide and Seek Whistle Letter Skills- Letter S box Math Skills- 7 Silly Snakes rhyme Color/Shape- White Cottonball	
Story Time	Read book:	Read book	Read book:	Read book:	
Game Time/Music	Music - Musical Instruments	Game - Play "I Spy"	Music – Sing, "Oh Be Careful Little Eyes What you See."	Game - Guess the Sound	
Closing Circle	Review today's theme, letter and math skills, color and shape	Review today's theme, letter and math skills, color and shape	Review today's theme, letter and math skills, color and shape	Review today's theme, letter and math skills, color and shape	Review this week's theme, letter, math, color, shape Pass out Care Bear backpack & Star Student briefcase

Suggestions:
Visit a bakery
Visit optomitrist

Weekly Lesson Plan — Theme: Terrific Teeth

Small Group Time:
1. Letter Skills
2. Numbers/Readiness Skills
3. Art or Cooking

	Monday	Tuesday	Wednesday	Thursday	Friday
Bible Time	Read Bible verse Tell Story of	Review Bible verse Prayer Time (use small white board to record/erase requests and praises)	Review Bible verse Prayer Time	Review Bible verse Prayer Time	Review Bible story Review Bible verse Prayer Time
Greeting Circle	Star Student Read Care Bear Journal Class Jobs Calendar/Weather Routine Birthdays & Share Bears (4)	Good Morning song Calendar/Weather Routine Birthdays Share Bears (4)	Good Morning song Calendar/Weather Routine Birthdays Share Bears (4)	Good Morning song Calendar/Weather Routine Birthdays Share Bears (4)	Good Morning song Calendar/Weather Routine Birthdays Share Bears (4)
Center Time/ Small Group Time	1. Decorate blank T with torn bits of colorful paper 2. Teeth Collecting (see Color) 3. Alligator Teeth	1. T is for Train Tracks 2. Counting Teeth (see Math) 3. Paint with Toothbrushes	1. T is for Toothbrush 2. Bank (see Math) 3. Tooth Fairy Bag	1. no activity today 2. Crown Jewels (see Shape) 3. Cooking: Marshmallow Smile	F I E
Circle Time	Theme- What are teeth made of? Letter Skills-Intro. Letter T Math Skills-Repeat the pattern Color/Shape-Walk Around the Diamond	Theme- Taking Care of Teeth Letter Skills- Ticking Clock game Math Skills- Count 7 Teeth Color/Shape-I Spy White	Theme-Colorful Stained Teeth Letter Skills- Pulling Teeth game Math Skills- Kangaroo Counting Color/Shape-Tooth Fairy Who has your Tooth?	Theme-How many teeth? Letter Skills- Letter T box Math Skills- Number Flashcard Review Color/Shape- Review all shapes using flashcards	L D T R I P
Story Time	Read book:	Read book:	Read book:	Read book:	
Game Time/Music	Game - Feed the Monster	Game - Soda Bottle Bowling	Music - Baby Bottle Shakers	Music - Train Follow the Leader	Suggestions: Visit a dentist Have hygienist visit Watch Arthur's Tooth
Closing Circle	Review today's theme, letter and math skills, color and shape	Review today's theme, letter and math skills, color and shape	Review today's theme, letter and math skills, color and shape	Review today's theme, letter and math skills, color and shape	Review this week's theme, letter, math, color, shape Pass out Care Bear backpack & Star Student briefcase

Weekly Lesson Plan   Theme: Special Holiday: Easter

Letter: review   Number: review   Scripture:
Color: white   Shape: diamond   Rom. 3:23

Small Group Time:
1.Letter Skills
2.Numbers/Readiness Skills
3-Art or Cooking

	Monday	Tuesday	Wednesday	Thursday	Friday
Bible Time	Read Bible verse Tell Story of Resurrection Eggs	Review Bible verse Prayer Time (use small white board to record/erase requests and praises)	Review Bible verse Prayer Time	Review Bible verse Prayer Time	Review Bible story Review Bible verse Prayer Time
Greeting Circle	Star Student Read Care Bear Journal Class Jobs Calendar/Weather Routine Birthdays & Share Bears (4)	Good Morning song Calendar/Weather Routine Birthdays Share Bears (4)	Good Morning song Calendar/Weather Routine Birthdays Share Bears (4)	Good Morning song Calendar/Weather Routine Birthdays Share Bears (4)	Good Morning song Calendar/Weather Routine Birthdays Share Bears (4)
Center/ Small Group Time	1. Trace alphabet magnets 2. no activity today 3. Make Resurrection Eggs	1.Alphabet stamping 2. no activity today 3. Easter Buckets	1.Playdough with alphabet cookie cutters 2. no activity today 3. Die Easter Eggs	1.no activity today 2.Decoupage Eggs (see Art) 3.Cooking: Resurrection Rolls	F I E L D T R I P
Circle Time	Theme- Triumphal Entry Letter Skills-What's the Sound song Math Skills-What Comes After game Color/Shape- Jump On Color game	Theme- Last Supper-/Jesus Washes the Disciples Feet Letter Skills-Sing Alphabet song Math Skills- Fishing for Numbers Color/Shape- Play I Spy	Theme- Jesus Prays In the Garden Letter Skills-Erase the letter Math Skills- Flashlight Writing Color/Shape-Stand up if you have on ___ game	Theme-Crucifixtion and Resurrection Letter Skills-Pick a Pocket Math Skills- Who Has # ___game Color/Shape-review with flashcards	
Story Time	Read book:	Read book:	Read book:	Read book:	
Game Time/Music	Game – Bunny Pokey	Music – Jelly Bean Shakers	Game – Bunny Hop Relay	Music – Happy Easter to You (like Happy Birthday)& We Wish You a Happy Easter	Suggestions: Have parents come for 'Thanksgiving Meal
Closing Circle	Review today's theme, letter and math skills, color and shape	Review today's theme, letter and math skills, color and shape	Review today's theme, letter and math skills, color and shape	Review today's theme, letter and math skills, color and shape	Review this week's theme, letter, math, color, shape Pass out Care Bear backpack & Star Student briefcase

Weekly Lesson Plan

Theme: Umbrellas/ Spring Showers and Other Signs of Spring

Small Group Time:
1.Letter Skills
2.Numbers/Readiness Skills
3-Art or Cooking

Letter:	U	Number:	8	Scripture:
Color:	black	Shape:	octagon	Gen. 9:13

	Monday	Tuesday	Wednesday	Thursday	Friday
Bible Time	Read Bible verse Tell Story of Noah	Review Bible verse Prayer Time (use small white board to record/erase requests and praises)	Review Bible verse Prayer Time	Review Bible verse Prayer Time	Review Bible story Review Bible verse Prayer Time
Greeting Circle	Star Student Read Care Bear Journal Class Jobs Calendar/Weather Routine Birthdays & Share Bears (4)	Good Morning song Calendar/Weather Routine Birthdays Share Bears (4)	Good Morning song Calendar/Weather Routine Birthdays Share Bears (4)	Good Morning song Calendar/Weather Routine Birthdays Share Bears (4)	Good Morning song Calendar/Weather Routine Birthdays Share Bears (4)
Center Time/ Small Group Time	1. Decorate blank U with fingerprint raindrops 2. Colorful Rainbow (see Bible) 3. Coffee Filter Umbrella	1.Letter U Water Color Painting 2. 8 Blades of Grass 3. Cupcake Liner Flower	1.U Macaroni picture 2. Black Storm Clouds painting (see Color) 3. Spring Windsock	1.no activity today 2. Flower Stickers (see Math) 3. Cooking: Blue Jello Sky with Cool Whip Clouds	F I E L D T R I P
Circle Time	Theme- Discuss signs of Spring Letter Skills-Intro. Letter U Math Skills-Intro. number 8 Color/Shape-Intro. black/octagon	Theme- Disc. Weather in Spring Letter Skills- U says "u" (poke tummy) Math Skills- Count the Flowers Color/Shape-	Theme-What Makes the Rain? Letter Skills- Math Skills- Straw Counters Color/Shape-Spring Binoculars	Theme-Discuss Spring Planting Letter Skills- Letter U box Math Skills- In My Garden sheet Color/Shape- Color Song (see Color)	
Story Time	Read book:	Read book:	Read book:	Read book:	
Game Time/Music	Music - "If all the Raindrops Were..." song	Game - Puddle Jumping	Game - Nature Walk-look for signs of Spring	Game - Baby Chick Hatches	Suggestions: Visit a farm Visit a flower nursery Have farmer or florist visit
Closing Circle	Review today's theme, letter and math skills, color and shape	Review today's theme, letter and math skills, color and shape	Review today's theme, letter and math skills, color and shape	Review today's theme, letter and math skills, color and shape	Review this week's theme, letter, math, color, shape Pass out Care Bear backpack & Star Student briefcase

Weekly Lesson Plan

Theme: Vroom, Vroom, Things that Go

Small Group Time:
1. Letter Skills
2. Numbers/Readiness Skills
3. Art or Cooking

Letter: V   Number: 8   Scripture:
Color: black   Shape: octagon   John 14:6

	Monday	Tuesday	Wednesday	Thursday	Friday
Bible Time	Read Bible verse Tell Story of the Tower of Babel	Review Bible verse Prayer Time (use small white board to record/erase requests and praises)	Review Bible verse Prayer Time	Review Bible verse Prayer Time	Review Bible story Review Bible verse Prayer Time
Greeting Circle	Star Student Read Care Bear Journal Class Jobs Calendar/Weather Routine Birthdays & Share Bears (4)	Good Morning song Calendar/Weather Routine Birthdays Share Bears (4)	Good Morning song Calendar/Weather Routine Birthdays Share Bears (4)	Good Morning song Calendar/Weather Routine Birthdays Share Bears (4)	Good Morning song Calendar/Weather Routine Birthdays Share Bears (4)
Center Time/ Small Group Time	1. Decorate blank V with car tracks 2. 8 Violin Strings 3. School Bus Collage	1. V is for Vegetables collage 2. Crayon Rubbing of License Plate 3. Paper Airplanes	1. Letter V - Map 2. 8 Wheels 3. Paper Plate Boat	1. no activity today 2. 8 Planets sheet 3. Cooking: Stop Light Snack	F I E
Circle Time	Theme- Modes of transportation - land vehicles Letter Skills- Intro. letter V Math Skills- Count 8 cars Color/Shape- Stop Sign game (see Shape)	Theme- Modes of transportation - air vehicles Letter Skills- Two Lane Road game Math Skills- Count 8 Keys Color/Shape- I Spy Black (see Color)	Theme- Modes of transportation - water vehicles Letter Skills- V - Vroom game Math Skills- Train Whistle Counting Color/Shape-Colorful Airplanes	Theme-Modes of transportation - outer space Letter Skills- Letter V box Math Skills - Roll the Planet Counting Color/Shape-Review shapes with flashcards	L D T R I P
Story Time	Read book:	Read book:	Read book:	Read book:	
Game Time/Music	Music - Freeze	Game - Red Light/Green Light	Music - Sing The Wheels on the Bus	Game - Paper Airplane Race	Suggestions: Visit car lot Visit local airport
Closing Circle	Review today's theme, letter and math skills, color and shape	Review today's theme, letter and math skills, color and shape	Review today's theme, letter and math skills, color and shape	Review today's theme, letter and math skills, color and shape	Review this week's theme, letter, math, color, shape Pass out Care Bear backpack & Star Student briefcase

Weekly Lesson Plan Theme: Wiggly, Crawly Things

Letter: W   Number: 8   Scripture:
Color: black   Shape: octagon   Prov. 6:6

Small Group Time:
1. Letter Skills
2. Numbers/Readiness Skills
3. Art or Cooking

	Monday	Tuesday	Wednesday	Thursday	Friday
Bible Time	Read Bible verse Tell Story of the Story of the Ant	Review Bible verse Prayer Time (use small white board to record/erase requests and praises)	Review Bible verse Prayer Time	Review Bible verse Prayer Time	Review Bible story Review Bible verse Prayer Time
Greeting Circle	Star Student Read Care Bear Journal Class Jobs Calendar/Weather Routine Birthdays & Share Bears (4)	Good Morning song Calendar/Weather Routine Birthdays Share Bears (4)	Good Morning song Calendar/Weather Routine Birthdays Share Bears (4)	Good Morning song Calendar/Weather Routine Birthdays Share Bears (4)	Good Morning song Calendar/Weather Routine Birthdays Share Bears (4)
Center Time/ Small Group Time	1. Decorate blank W with "worms" - pieces of yarn 2. Measure the Worm 3. Coffee Filter Butterfly	1. W is for Wiggly Worm (see Color) 2. Sandpaper Rubbing (see Shape) 3. Caterpillar Egg Carton	1. W is for Web (see Color) 2. 8 Insect Stickers 3. Spider Hat (see Art)	1. no activity today 2. Bumblebee Number 8 3. Cooking: Ladybug Jigglers	F I E L D
Circle Time	Theme- List the Insects Letter Skills- Intro. letter W Math Skills- Yard Stick Bug Pick Up game Color/Shape-Circle insects that are black from list during Theme time	Theme- Disc. How they Help Us Letter Skills- W is for Worm Math Skills- 8 Dots on a Ladybug game Color/Shape- Stop Sign Bug game (see Shape)	Theme- From Caterpillar to Butterfly Letter Skills- W is for Watermelon Math Skills- Spiders Have 8 Legs. Color/Shape-Talk about what color seeds are in the watermelon above	Theme-Disc. Ants Letter Skills- Letter W box Math Skills- The Ants Go Marching song (see Music) Color/Shape-Review colors using flashcards	T R I P
Story Time	Read book:	Read book:	Read book:	Read book:	Suggestions: Guest - disc. composting Guest - Bee Keeper Watch Magic Schoolbus or A Bug's Life
Game Time/Music	Music - Move Like A ___	Game - Mosquito Tag	Music - Bumblebee Dance	Music - Itsy Bitsy Spider	
Closing Circle	Review today's theme, letter and math skills, color and shape	Review today's theme, letter and math skills, color and shape	Review today's theme, letter and math skills, color and shape	Review today's theme, letter and math skills, color and shape	Review this week's theme, letter, math, color, shape Pass out Care Bear backpack & Star Student briefcase

Weekly Lesson Plan   Theme: X-rays and Bones

Letter: X Color: black Number: 8 Shape: octagon Scripture: Eph. 2:10

Small GroupTime:
1. Letter Skills
2. Numbers/Readiness Skills
3- Art or Cooking

	Monday	Tuesday	Wednesday	Thursday	Friday
Bible Time	Read Bible verse Tell Story of Samson	Review Bible verse Prayer Time (use small white board to record/erase requests and praises)	Review Bible verse Prayer Time	Review Bible verse Prayer Time	Review Bible story Review Bible verse Prayer Time
Greeting Circle	Star Student Read Care Bear Journal Class Jobs Calendar/Weather Routine Birthdays & Share Bears (4)	Good Morning song Calendar/Weather Routine Birthdays Share Bears (4)	Good Morning song Calendar/Weather Routine Birthdays Share Bears (4)	Good Morning song Calendar/Weather Routine Birthdays Share Bears (4)	Good Morning song Calendar/Weather Routine Birthdays Share Bears (4)
Center Time/ Small Group Time	1. Decorate blank X like a xylophone 2. Bone Counting (see Math) 3. Milk Jug Skelton	1. Q-tip Skeleton (see Art) 2. French Fry Counting (see Math) 3. Continue Milk Jug Skeleton	1. X Bones 2. Make X-ray (see Color) 3. Greeting Card Collage	1. no activity today 2. Dig Up 8 Buried Skeltons 3. Cooking: Ladybug Jigglers	F I E
Circle Time	Theme- X-ray/Our Bones Letter Skills-Intro, letter X. Math Skills-Count 8 bones Color/Shape-Look at real X-ray (see Color)	Theme- Our Skeleton Letter Skills- Xylophone practice. Math Skills- Bone Patterns Color/Shape- X-Ray glasses - look for black (see Color)	Theme- Movement/Protectors Letter Skills-X says "ks" Math Skills- Elevator Counting Color/Shape-Traffic Sign Patterns	Theme- Strong Bones Letter Skills- XOXO game Math Skills- Review numbers using flashcards Color/Shape-Feel the Shape	L D T
Story Time	Read book:	Read book:	Read book:	Read book:	R I P
Game Time/Music	Music - Bone Pokey	Game - Skeleton, Skeleton, Where's Your Bone	Music - X-ray (like Freeze)	Game - Xerox Game	Suggestions: Visit orthopedist Watch The Magic Schoolbus-Inside the Human Body
Closing Circle	Review today's theme, letter and math skills, color and shape	Review today's theme, letter and math skills, color and shape	Review today's theme, letter and math skills, color and shape	Review today's theme, letter and math skills, color and shape	Review this week's theme, letter, math, color, shape Pass out Care Bear backpack & Star Student briefcase

Weekly Lesson Plan

Theme: Yippee, Summer is Here

		Letter: Y	Number: 9	Scripture:
		Color: purple	Shape: oval	Gen. 1:16

Small Group Time:
1. Letter Skills
2. Numbers/Readiness Skills
3. Art or Cooking

	Monday	Tuesday	Wednesday	Thursday	Friday
Bible Time	Read Bible verse Tell Story of God Made Two Great Lights	Review Bible verse Prayer Time (use small white board to record/erase requests and praises)	Review Bible verse Prayer Time	Review Bible verse Prayer Time	Review Bible story Review Bible verse Prayer Time
Greeting Circle	Star Student Read Care Bear Journal Class Jobs Calendar/Weather Routine Birthdays & Share Bears (4)	Good Morning song Calendar/Weather Routine Birthdays Share Bears (4)	Good Morning song Calendar/Weather Routine Birthdays Share Bears (4)	Good Morning song Calendar/Weather Routine Birthdays Share Bears (4)	Good Morning song Calendar/Weather Routine Birthdays Share Bears (4)
Center Time/ Small Group Time	1. Decorate blank Y with yarn 2. Sun Print Oval (see Shape) 3. Sun Catcher	1. Y is for Yellow like the Sun 2. Sunflower Seed Counting 3. Sea Shell Frame	1. Y is for Yam Stamping 2. Golf Ball Painting (see Color) 3. Summer Snow Globe	1. no activity today 2. Sandpaper Sandcastle 3. Cooking: Ocean and Sand Snack	F I E
Circle Time	Theme- Disc. Seasons Letter Skills-Intro. letter Y Math Skills-Intro. number 9 Color/Shape-Show a Yam, discuss it's shape (oval)	Theme- Discuss Summer Activities Letter Skills-Yam Toss Math Skills- Beach Ball Numbers Color/Shape- Seeing Purple	Theme- Discuss Summer Vacations Letter Skills-Yell for Letter Y Math Skills- Sea Shell Counting Color/Shape-Pass the Oval	Theme- Discuss Temperature Letter Skills- Letter Y box Math Skills- Beach Ball Counting Color/Shape-Review shapes using flashcards	L D T
Story Time	Read book:	Read book:	Read book:	Read book:	R I P
Game Time/Music	Music – song, "You are My Sunshine" (with hand puppets)	Game – Bubbles	Music – Soda Bottle Shakers	Game – Freeze Tag	Suggestions: Water Fun Day (see Games)
Closing Circle	Review today's theme, letter and math skills, color and shape	Review today's theme, letter and math skills, color and shape	Review today's theme, letter and math skills, color and shape	Review today's theme, letter and math skills, color and shape	Review this week's theme, letter, math, color, shape Pass out Care Bear backpack & Star Student briefcase

Weekly Lesson Plan   Theme: Zoo

Letter: Z | Color: purple | Number: 10 | Shape: oval | Scripture: Luke 19:10

Small Group Time:
1.Letter Skills
2.Numbers/Readiness Skills
3-Art or Cooking

	Monday	Tuesday	Wednesday	Thursday	Friday
Bible Time	Read Bible verse Tell Story of Zachaeus	Review Bible verse Prayer Time (use small white board to record/erase requests and praises)	Review Bible verse Prayer Time	Review Bible verse Prayer Time	Review Bible story Review Bible verse Prayer Time
Greeting Circle	Star Student Read Care Bear Journal Class Jobs Calendar/Weather Routine Birthdays & Share Bears (4)	Good Morning song Calendar/Weather Routine Birthdays Share Bears (4)	Good Morning song Calendar/Weather Routine Birthdays Share Bears (4)	Good Morning song Calendar/Weather Routine Birthdays Share Bears (4)	Good Morning song Calendar/Weather Routine Birthdays Share Bears (4)
Center Time/ Small Group Time	1. Decorate blank Z with Zebra Stripes 2. no activity today 3. Sycamore Tree (see Bible)	1.Zoo Animal Play Dough 2. Animal Cracker Counters 3. Zebra Stripes	1.Z is for Zucchini 2. Teddy Graham Counters 3. Giraffe that Stands	1.no activity today 2. Feed the Animals Toss 3.Cooking: Banana Split	F I E L D T R I P
Circle Time	Theme- What is a zoo? Letter Skills-Intro. letter Z Math Skills-Zoo Animal Patterns Color/Shape-Show red and blue make purple	Theme- Animals in the Zoo Letter Skills-Z is for Zipping game Math Skills- Sing 5 Little Monkies (see Music) Color/Shape- Oval Bear	Theme- Zoo Animals' Needs Letter Skills- Math Skills- Barrel of Monkies Counting Color/Shape-Color Patterns	Theme-Zoo Keeper/Veterinarian Letter Skills-Letter Z box Math Skills- Review numbers 1-10 Color/Shape-Review shapes learned this year	
Story Time	Read book:	Read book:	Read book:	Read book:	
Game Time/Music	Music – The Animals in the Zoo song	Game - Zoo Keeper May I (like Mother May I)	Game – Pass the Bear (like Hot Potato)	Game - Monkey, Monkey, Bear (Like Duck, Cuck, Goose)	Suggestions: Visit the zoo Have last day party
Closing Circle	Review today's theme, letter and math skills, color and shape	Review today's theme, letter and math skills, color and shape	Review today's theme, letter and math skills, color and shape	Review today's theme, letter and math skills, color and shape	Review this week's theme, letter, math, color, shape Pass out Care Bear backpack & Star Student briefcase

Resources
&
Black Line Masters

The First Christmas Reindeer

I am a Christmas Reindeer.
I was grazing on a hill
When an angel appeared overhead.
It seemed the world stood still.
Shepherds who had seen the sight
Passed by me as they sang,
We're going to see the Son of God,
Who will forever reign.
At long last, we had arrived.
Our journey led us to a trough.
There we beheld a wondrous sight,
Baby Jesus-wrapped in swaddling cloth.
I was so moved by what I saw.
I wanted all to know.
So I began to run and run,
But, my legs just seemed too slow.
Then suddenly my legs felt light.
I was floating through the air.
It seemed I was now flying.
All below just looked and stared.
I sang out as I flew around,
God's only Son's been born.
He came to save the world from sin,
To rescue sin-sick and forlorn.
This is the story of how I became
A deer with wings it seems.
I still fly around all over
And of His praise I sing.
Merry Christmas!

The First Christmas Reindeer

I am a Christmas Reindeer.
I was grazing on a hill
When an angel appeared overhead.
It seemed the world stood still.
Shepherds who had seen the sight
Passed by me as they sang,
We're going to see the Son of God,
Who will forever reign.
At long last, we had arrived.
Our journey led us to a trough.
There we beheld a wondrous sight,
Baby Jesus-wrapped in swaddling cloth.
I was so moved by what I saw.
I wanted all to know.
So I began to run and run,
But, my legs just seemed too slow.
Then suddenly my legs felt light.
I was floating through the air.
It seemed I was now flying.
All below just looked and stared.
I sang out as I flew around,
God's only Son's been born.
He came to save the world from sin,
To rescue sin-sick and forlorn.
This is the story of how I became
A deer with wings it seems.
I still fly around all over
And of His praise I sing.
Merry Christmas!

The First Christmas Reindeer

I am a Christmas Reindeer.
I was grazing on a hill
When an angel appeared overhead.
It seemed the world stood still.
Shepherds who had seen the sight
Passed by me as they sang,
We're going to see the Son of God,
Who will forever reign.
At long last, we had arrived.
Our journey led us to a trough.
There we beheld a wondrous sight,
Baby Jesus-wrapped in swaddling cloth.
I was so moved by what I saw.
I wanted all to know.
So I began to run and run,
But, my legs just seemed too slow.
Then suddenly my legs felt light.
I was floating through the air.
It seemed I was now flying.
All below just looked and stared.
I sang out as I flew around,
God's only Son's been born.
He came to save the world from sin,
To rescue sin-sick and forlorn.
This is the story of how I became
A deer with wings it seems.
I still fly around all over
And of His praise I sing.
Merry Christmas!

The First Christmas Reindeer

I am a Christmas Reindeer.
I was grazing on a hill
When an angel appeared overhead.
It seemed the world stood still.
Shepherds who had seen the sight
Passed by me as they sang,
We're going to see the Son of God,
Who will forever reign.
At long last, we had arrived.
Our journey led us to a trough.
There we beheld a wondrous sight,
Baby Jesus-wrapped in swaddling cloth.
I was so moved by what I saw.
I wanted all to know.
So I began to run and run,
But, my legs just seemed too slow.
Then suddenly my legs felt light.
I was floating through the air.
It seemed I was now flying.
All below just looked and stared.
I sang out as I flew around,
God's only Son's been born.
He came to save the world from sin,
To rescue sin-sick and forlorn.
This is the story of how I became
A deer with wings it seems.
I still fly around all over
And of His praise I sing.
Merry Christmas!

HEART Bingo Directions:

Randomly call out the pictures listed below with any of the following letters: HEART

Valentine with lace
Bear with heart
Heart balloons
Blue candy
Purple, green candy
Red heart
Arrow
Green sucker
Red sucker
Envelope with heart
Mouse with heart
Heart with face

Copy this page and write the letter used beside each picture if you want to keep up with the ones you have already called out.

Use heart shaped Sweet Tarts for the tokens.

H E A R T

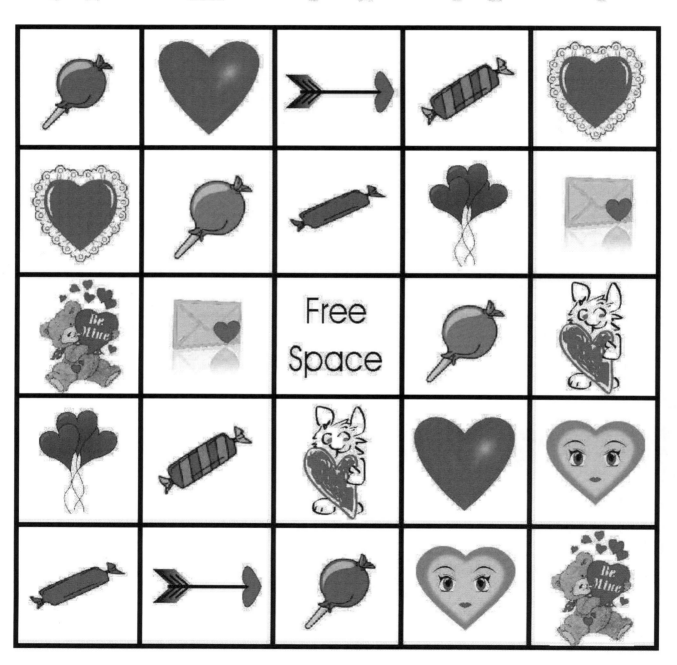

HEART

H E A R T

H E A R T

RESURRECTION EGGS

NAME: _____

RESURRECTION EGGS

NAME: _____

RESURRECTION EGGS

NAME: _____

Resurrection Eggs – papers that go inside each egg

Egg #1:

Message -- Jesus rode into Jerusalem on a donkey. The people waved palm branches.
Passage -- Matthew 21:1-11

Egg #2:

Message -- Jesus shared the Last Supper with His disciples.
Passage -- Matthew 26:17-19

Egg #3:

Message -- Jesus was nailed to a cross and pierced in His side. He died to take the punishment for our sins.
Passage -- John 19:18,37 & John 20:25-29

Egg #4:

Message -- Spices were used to prepare Jesus' body for burial.
Passage -- John 19:40

Egg #5:

Message -- The stone covering Jesus' tomb was rolled away.
Passage -- John 20:1

Egg #6:

Message -- The tomb was empty! Jesus was not there! He has risen!
Passage – Luke 24:6

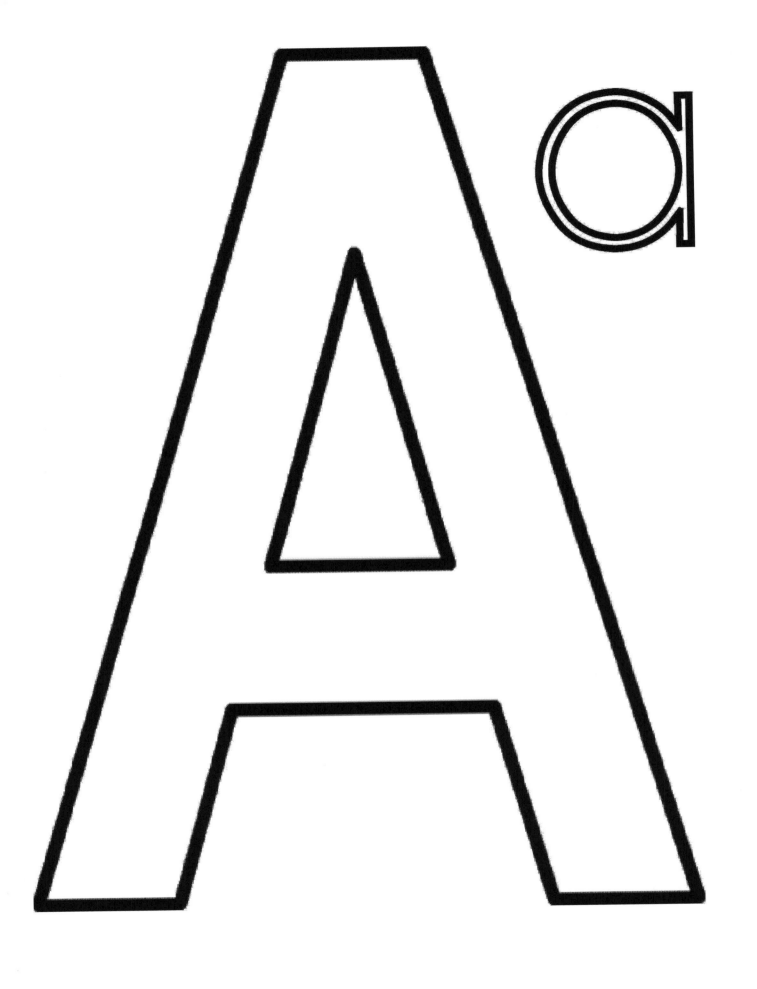

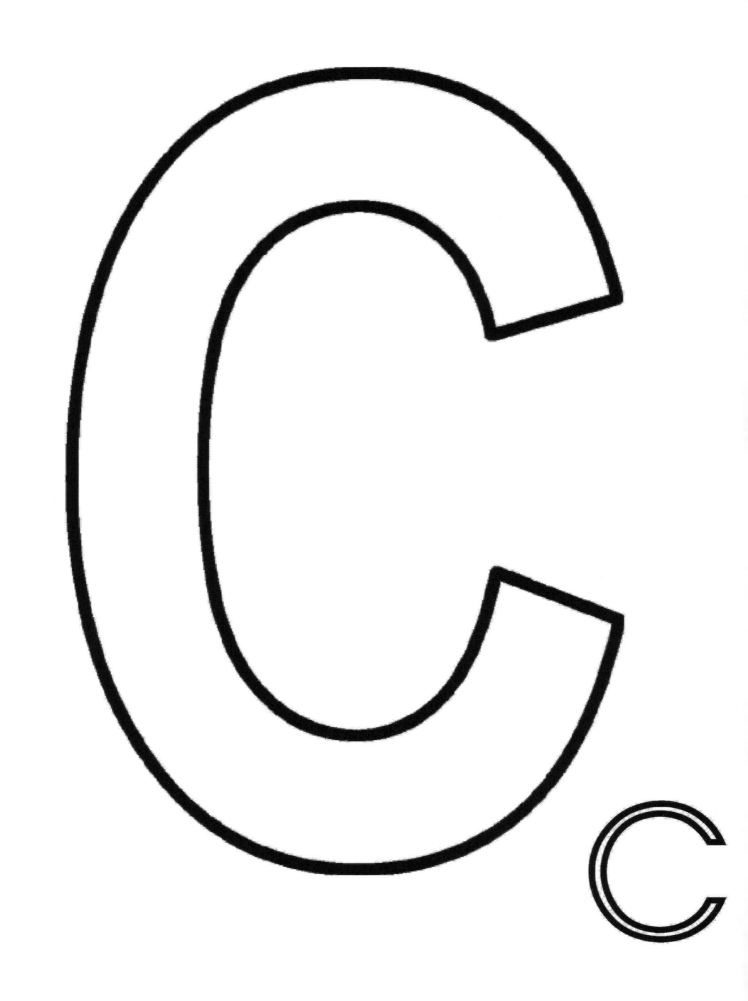

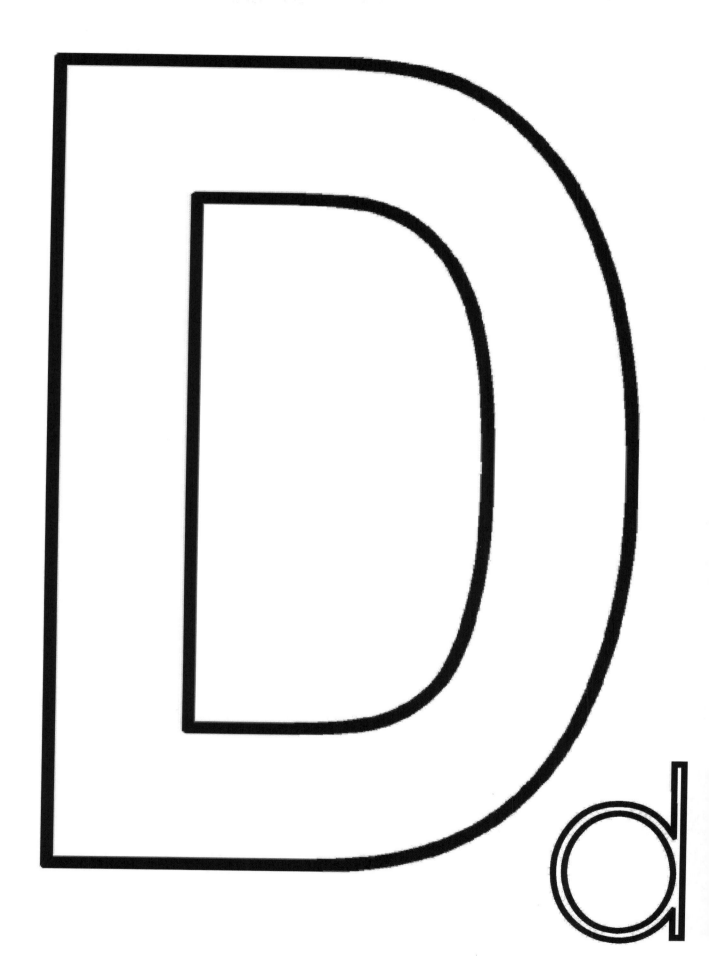

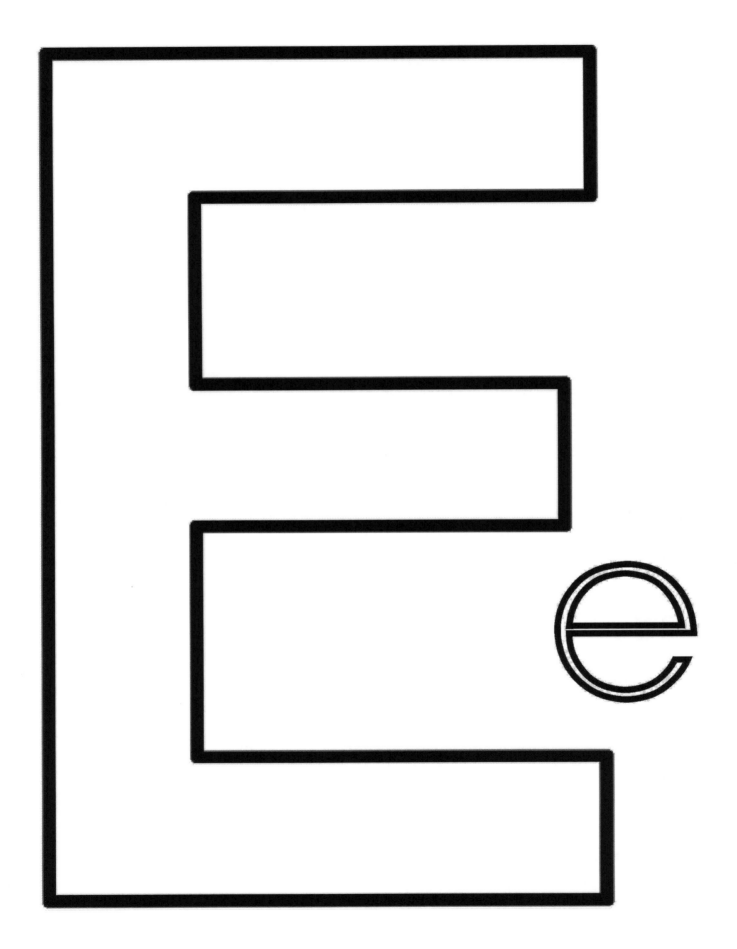

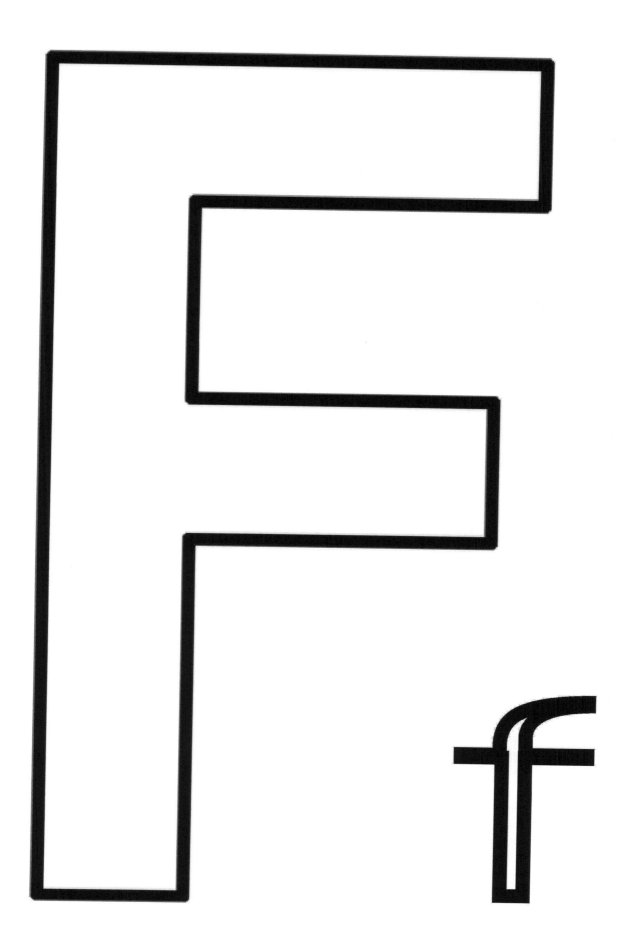

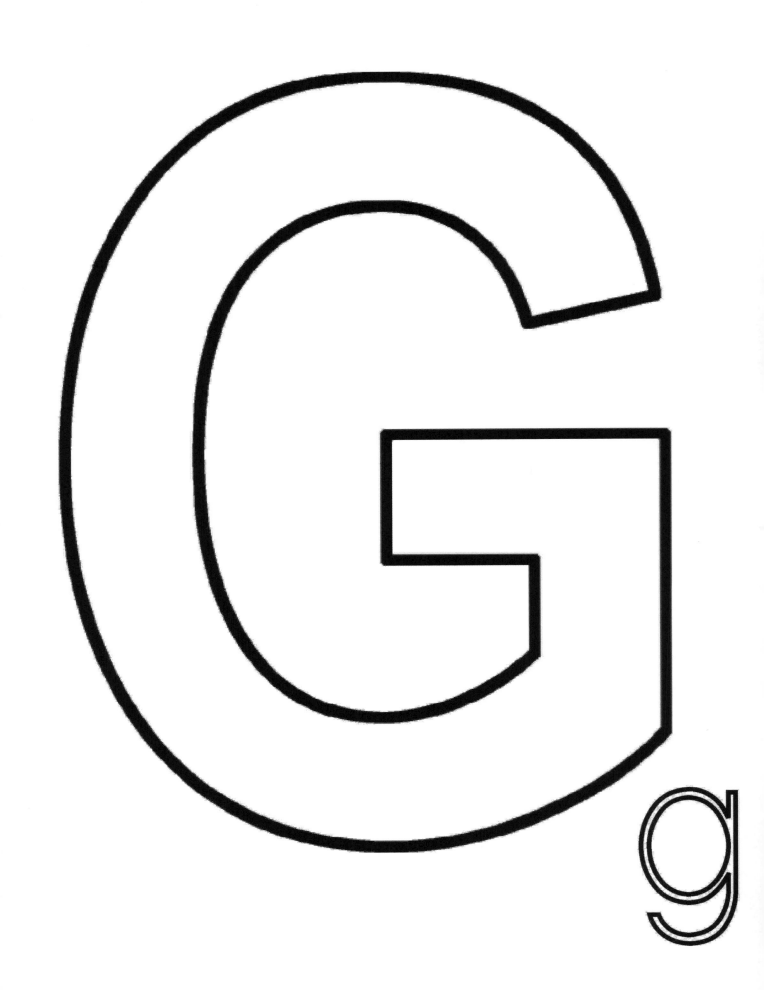

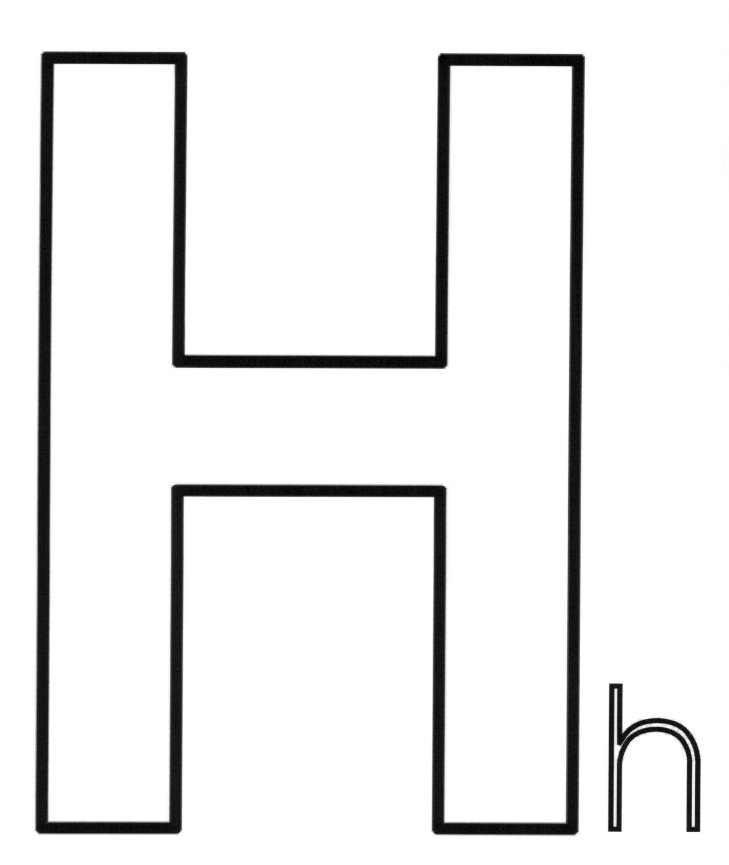

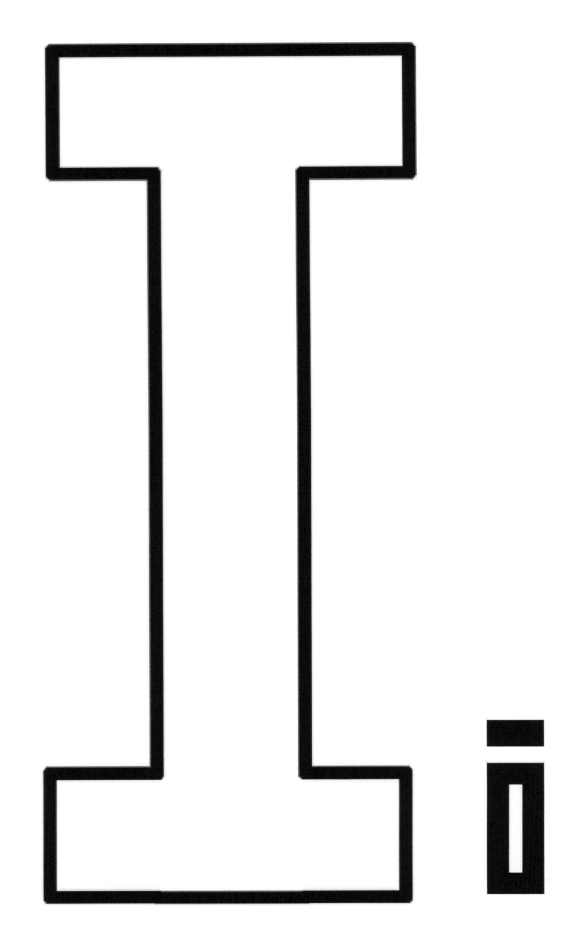

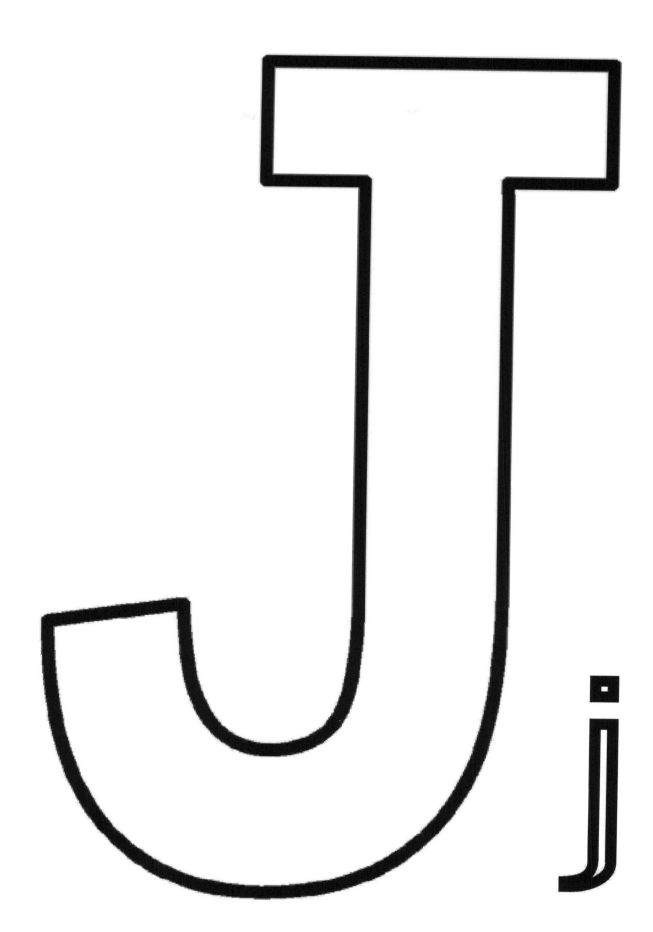

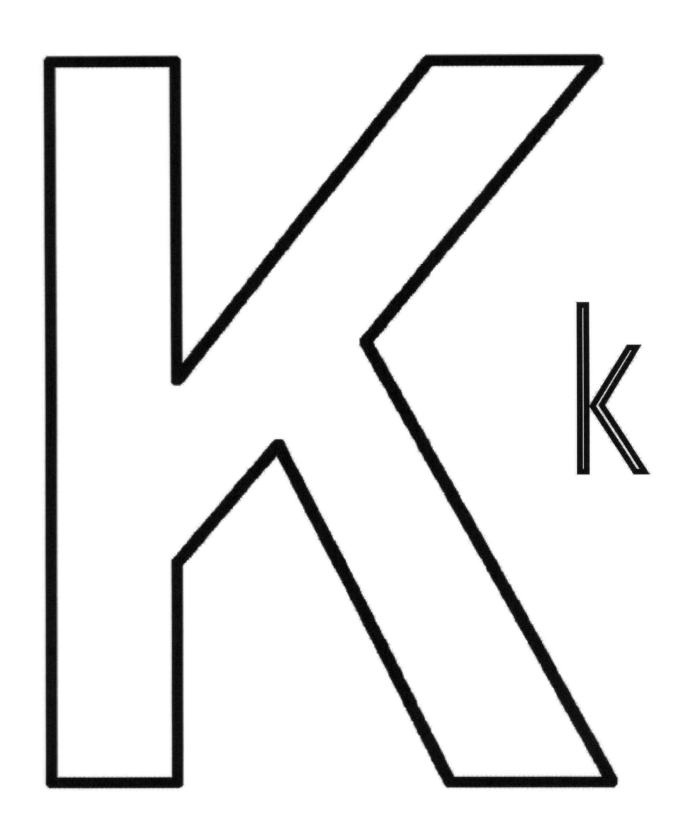

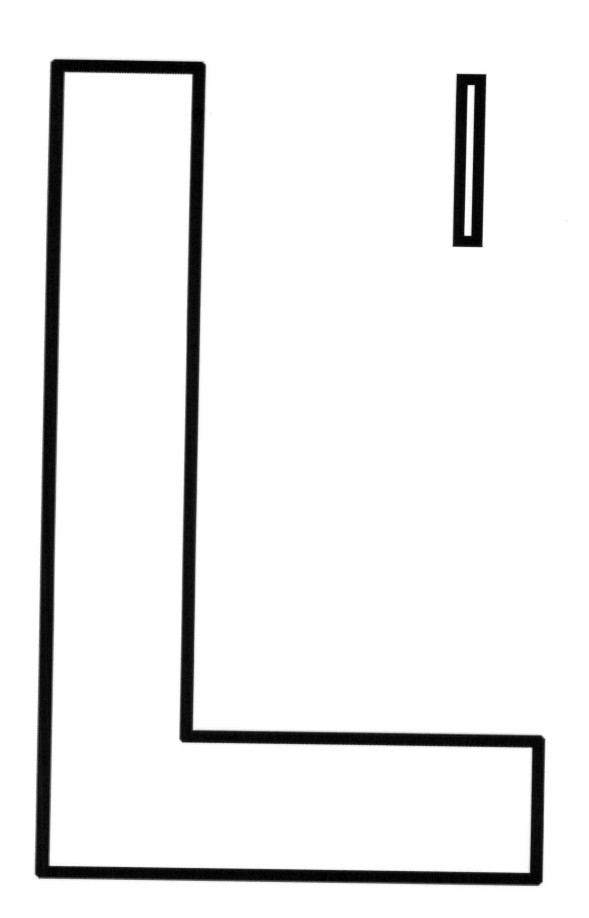

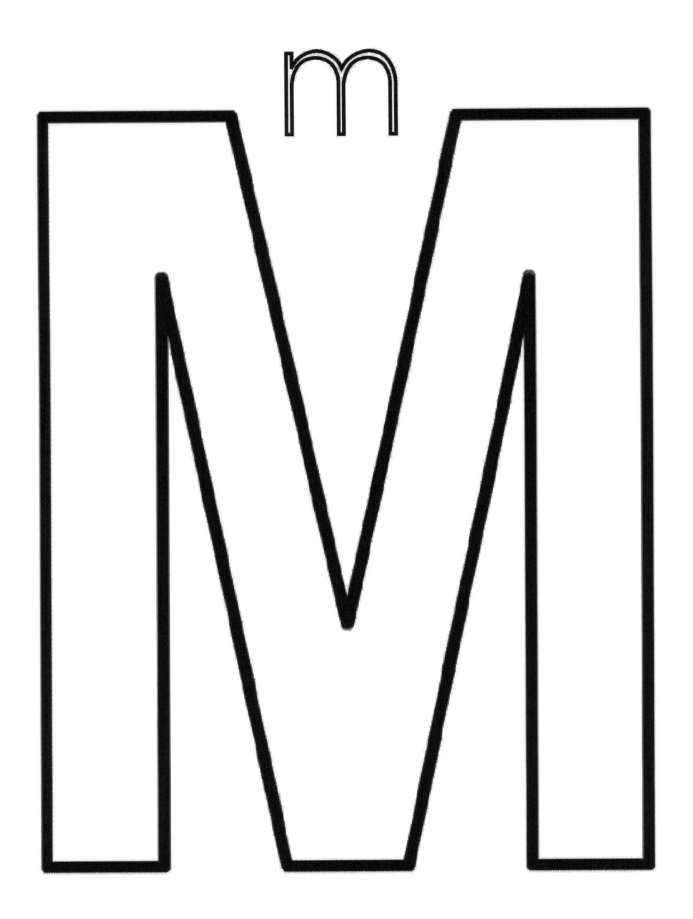

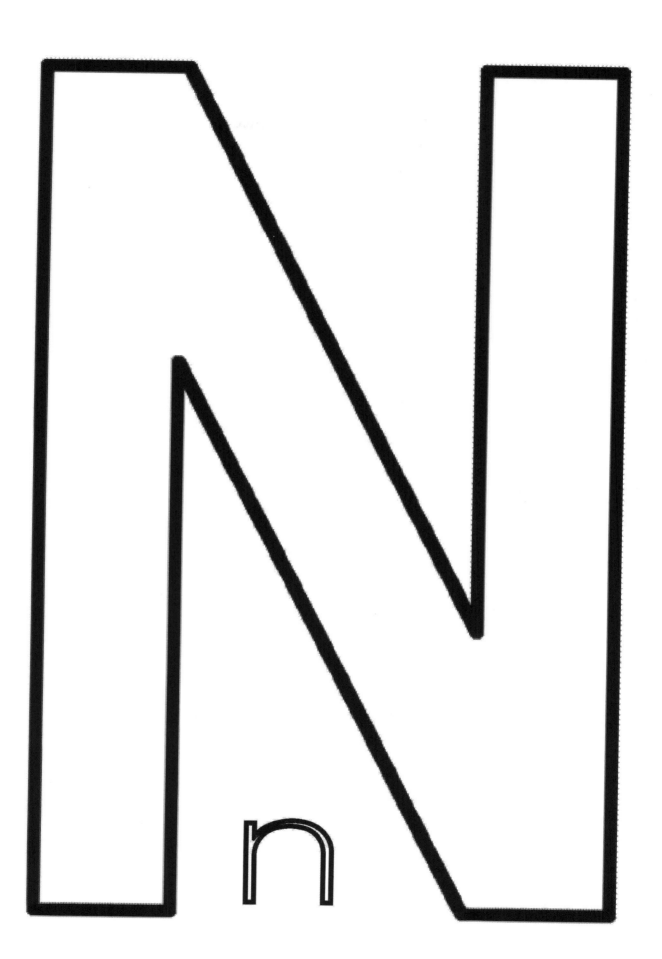

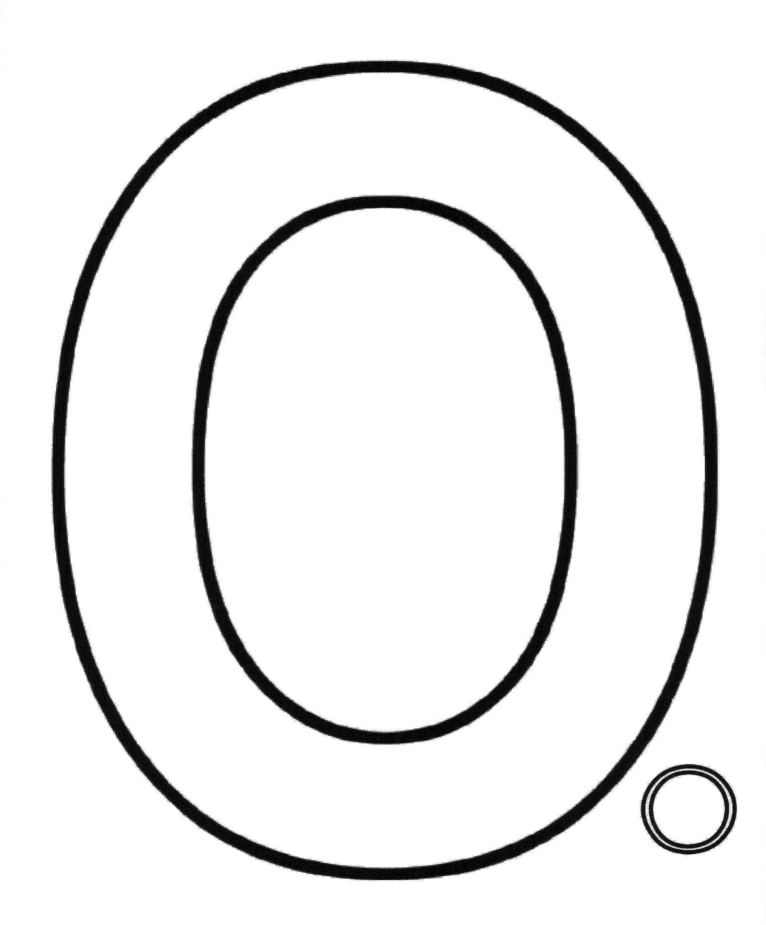

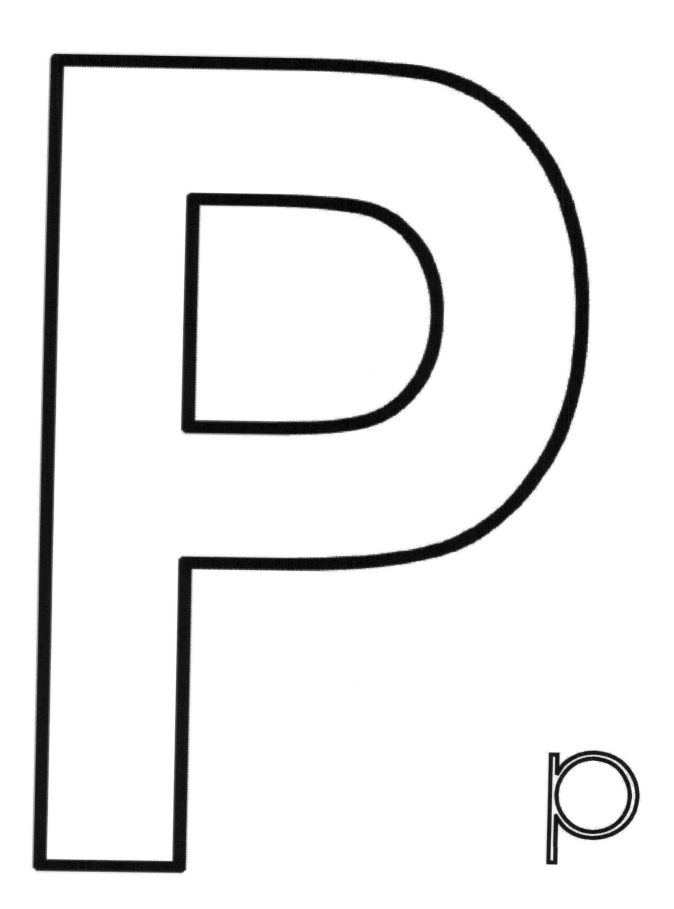

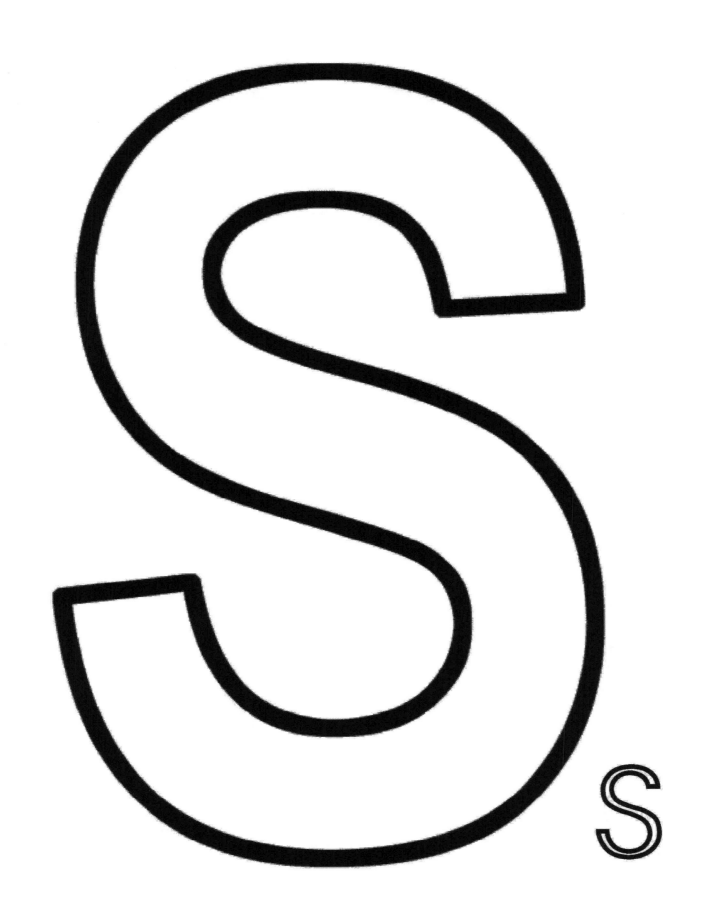

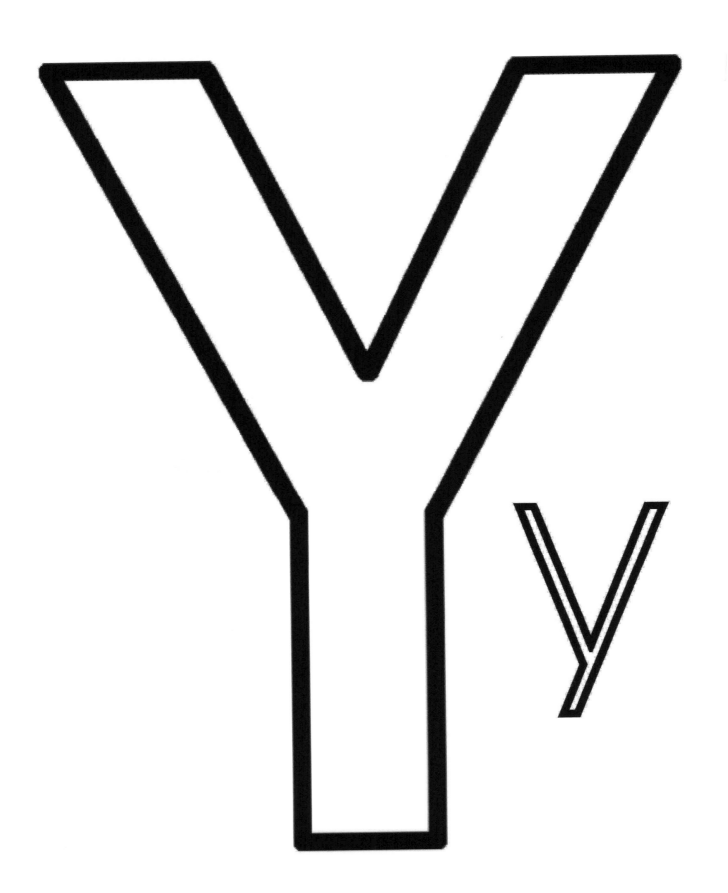

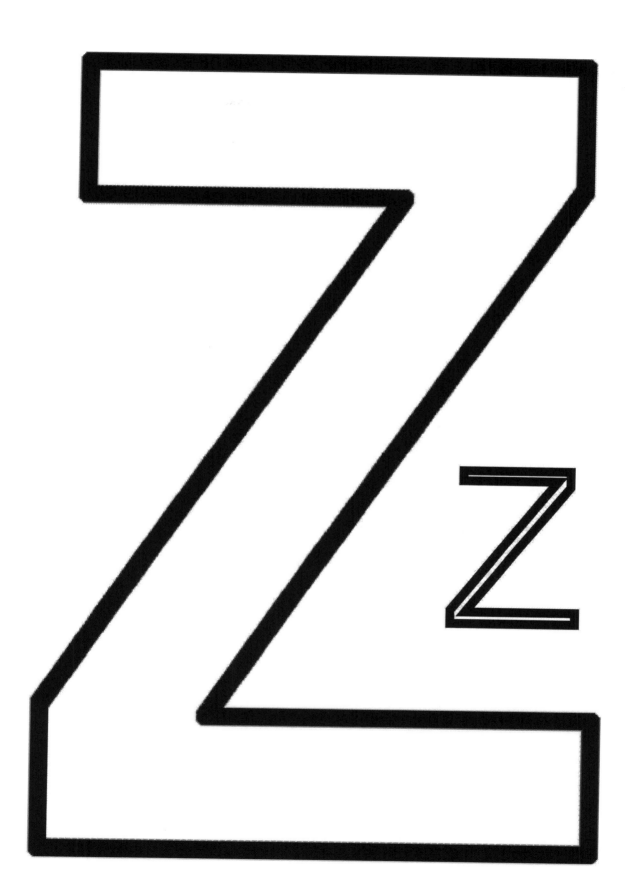

Made in the USA
Las Vegas, NV
09 September 2021